Copyright © 2018 Cathrine Dahl
All rights reserved.
ISBN: 978-82-93697-18-3

- Successful Dating -

No More Frogs

Get to know the

FEMALES

in the zodiac

by
Cathrine Dahl

CONTENTS

Page 1 | PREFACE: A few words about compatibility
and why traditional compatibility guides can give you the wrong idea

---

Get to know your date.
Blind Date, Speedy Essentials
• The Essence • Who's waiting for you? • Emergency fixes for embarrassing pauses • Your place or mine? • Checklist

Aries		5	Taurus		39	Gemini		73
Cancer		107	Leo		141	Virgo		175
Libra		209	Scorpio		243	Sagittarius		277
Capricorn		311	Aquarius		345	Pisces		379

CHAPTER 1: Prepare Yourself
• Top 10 Attention Grabbers • Her Dream Date; the essence of him • Her Arousal Meter

Aries		9	Taurus		43	Gemini		77
Cancer		111	Leo		145	Virgo		179
Libra		213	Scorpio		247	Sagittarius		281
Capricorn		315	Aquarius		349	Pisces		383

CHAPTER 2: The First Date
• Getting your foot in the door • Whatever you do, don't...
• Signs you're in – or not • Not your type? Making an exit

Aries		13	Taurus		47	Gemini		81
Cancer		115	Leo		149	Virgo		175
Libra		217	Scorpio		251	Sagittarius		285
Capricorn		319	Aquarius		353	Pisces		387

TIP: Don't always play by the book, play it by ear. Flexibility and spontaneity can create sparks - just be careful not to blow any fuses...

CHAPTER 3: Sex'n Stuff
• How to get her in the mood • Preferences and erotic nature
• Hitting the right buttons • Her expectations • Her vs. your erotic preferences

Aries	| 19	Taurus	| 53	Gemini	| 87
Cancer	| 121	Leo	| 155	Virgo	| 189
Libra	| 223	Scorpio	| 257	Sagittarius	| 291
Capricorn	| 325	Aquarius	| 359	Pisces	| 393

CHAPTER 4: The Big Picture
• Her personality - Pros and Cons • Romantic vibes • Erotic vibrations

Aries	| 25	Taurus	| 59	Gemini	| 93
Cancer	| 127	Leo	| 161	Virgo	| 195
Libra	| 229	Scorpio	| 263	Sagittarius	| 297
Capricorn	| 331	Aquarius	| 365	Pisces	| 399

CHAPTER 5: Compatibility Quiz

Aries	| 31	Taurus	| 65	Gemini	| 99
Cancer	| 133	Leo	| 167	Virgo	| 201
Libra	| 235	Scorpio	| 269	Sagittarius	| 303
Capricorn	| 337	Aquarius	| 371	Pisces	| 405

- Successful Dating -
No More Frogs

by Cathrine Dahl

No More Frogs - Successful Dating is your one-stop dating guide. No unnecessary blah-blah. The information is right here, at your fingertips.

This guide can be used in several ways. It's a handy tool when you want to prepare yourself a little. It can give you an advantage when going on a date or getting to know someone you've just met - or even someone you've known for a while.

Although this guide can help you angle your approach, remember to be true to yourself. Have fun, be wise, follow your heart - and keep your feet on the ground!

- Cathrine Dahl

Preface:
A few words about compatibility, and why compatibility guides can give you the wrong idea.

So you've met this Gemini you really, really like, but you're a Scorpio, and the compatibility guides say you're a lousy match. Guess what? That's rubbish!

Some compatibility guides offer a very simplistic approach, claiming that your best matches are the star signs within the same element as you:

Fire: Aries, Leo and Sagittarius
Earth: Taurus, Virgo and Capricorn
Air: Gemini, Libra and Aquarius
Water: Cancer, Scorpio and Pisces

Other guides are slightly more specific, declaring that we are compatible with star signs within our astrological polarity.

Yin: Taurus, Virgo, Capricorn, Cancer, Scorpio and Pisces
Yang: Aries, Leo, Sagittarius, Gemini, Libra and Aquarius

Doesn't look too good, does it? The most optimistic approach has removed half of the population from your dating pool. It doesn't make any sense. The true picture is far more promising...

One star sign, two very different personalities

Each of us has a unique astrological thumbprint determined by the sun, the moon and the planets. The most important factors being your ascending star (ascendant), the sun (star sign) and the moon (feelings).

Let's make it simple
Imagine your star sign being a melody. All the other aspects (the unique positioning of the moon and the planets) are sound effects, applied by a producer with a mixer.

The combination of rhythm, depth and base creates your unique sound. Another person with the same star sign will get his own sound mix and end up with a different beat.

Your personal melody can create wonderful harmonies with star signs you're not supposed to get on with – and nothing but noise with signs that are meant to be matches. You won't find out until you get to know each other.

Let's get to know your date...

ARIES the female

YOUR DATE: ARIES
21 March–20 April

The Essence of her

Energetic and enthusiastic – assertive in every aspect of her life – intelligent – strong, independent and confident – has a low tolerance for weakness, but defends those who do not have her strength – a good friend – enjoys a challenge, both professionally and personally – charming – lively – body-conscious and attractive – efficient; hates wasting time

...and remember: Don't be fooled by her pleasant and warm personality – this woman won't settle for a quiet life. The moment things start slowing down is when she will move on and make the next thing happen. Fasten your seatbelt.

Blind Date – speedy essentials

Who's waiting for you?
You'll probably get there at the same time she does. She'll be dashing out of a taxi with a big smile, telling you she had to finish painting her living room or finish a 100-page project – and 'Oh, by the way, where are we going from here?' She is direct and confident, and she will dazzle you with her charm and assertiveness. This energy will set the tone for the evening. If you'd planned an intimate dinner at a romantic bistro, you'd better rethink your agenda. As soon as you've recovered from the energetic hello, you'll notice her attractiveness... This is a very exciting woman.

Emergency fixes for embarrassing pauses.
Embarrassing pauses? These will occur for one of two reasons: either you are absolutely stunning, a Mr Universe who has rendered her speechless (this is virtually impossible), or you have failed to capture her interest (this is more likely). Don't worry. Her dates don't usually get this far. She will make an excuse and be off if she realises it's not a good match. On the other hand, if she likes you and suspects that you're the strong and silent type, your best bet is to be just that. Approach her with intelligent questions, but don't be too serious.

Your place or mine?
Either – or anywhere, for that matter. She is open to erotic adventures. She is also sexually assertive, and she won't wait for a man to make a move. If the chemistry is right and she finds her date attractive – strong, masculine and confident with a good body – moving from A to B comes naturally to her. Although she may be looking for a committed relationship, she doesn't mind if the date turns out to be a one-night stand.

Checklist, before you dash out to meet her:
Display something masculine and personal
(hint: something that has a story)
Prepare several options for how to spend the evening
(hint: make it exciting)
Make sure your wallet is full
(hint: take charge and pick up the bill)
Wear stylish attire that indicates a touch of success
(hint: an expensive shirt, watch or jacket, etc.)
Keep your cellphone turned on
(hint: let her see that you're an active guy)

Tip: She admires strength and masculinity – but if you try to impress her, keep it casual. 'This little scar? Oh, no big deal. I got it when … [fill in the blank with your most gutsy activity]'.

CHAPTER 1

PREPARE YOURSELF

Catch her eye, capture her attention
Top 10 attention grabbers

1. Be playful and tease her a little.
2. Wear something that shows off your masculinity. A t-shirt from an outdoor race or event would be an added bonus.
3. Be confident but a little reserved. Keep her guessing about your interest.
4. Let her see you surrounded by women before you divert your attention to her.
5. Good looks and nice attire are important.
6. Surprise her with one rose – not a dozen.
7. Make your date night active; a concert etc – rather than passive; watching a movie
8. Chose the restaurant based on the atmosphere and energy.
9. Be impulsive. Do something fun on the spur of the moment.
10. Embrace challenges with positivity.

The HE. The man!

The Aries woman can become completely absorbed by a strong and confident guy, especially if he seems disinterested! She'll treat a man who's not yet dazzled by her like a challenge. However, she does prefer attentive guys – strong attentive guys. She may fall for a macho guy, but her interest won't last unless he lives up to her expectations of sensitivity. Her perfect partner is independent, adventurous, ambitious and sensual. Most importantly, he must be able to keep up with her.

The Essence of him

Confident and strong – has a playful gleam in his eyes – physically active: the more adventurous, the better – energetic – ambitious – erotically impulsive – good-looking – loyal and supportive – independent and liberated, but faithful – has a good sense of humour – smart, but never patronising – positive and enthusiastic

Aries arousal meter

From 0 to 100... In five minutes, unless she's already off somewhere. She is easily turned on and doesn't mind giving into erotic feelings anytime and anywhere – well, almost. Scheduling sex is completely out of the question.

Remember: Be true to yourself
It doesn't matter if she is the most stunning girl you've ever met – if you don't match, you don't match. You may be able to put on a show for a while to hold her attention, but what's the point? We can't please everybody. We all have different needs, dreams, tastes and preferences. There's no such thing as a one-size-fits-all lover. Be yourself, and be true to who you are – always!

Very important: It's important to keep up her pace. Kicking back after work is seldom – or never – an option. Her energy is amazing. She will line up activities and expect you to tag along. If you're really not up for it, tell her straight.

CHAPTER 2

THE FIRST DATE

Getting your foot in the door
The basics

Keep it exciting. She loves trying new things. Take her to new places and introduce her to interesting people and exciting activities. Go ahead and suggest things that are a little out of the ordinary. The female Aries can be a daredevil and will love it if you have exciting ideas.

Step on it! ...or step aside. She dislikes boring people and will quickly shake you off if you can't keep up with her. If you want to capture her, fasten your seatbelt and step on it.

Display your masculinity. She is attracted to the strength in a man. If you want to win her heart – or get her into your bed – then draw attention to your masculine side. You won't capture her interest by being soft, gentle and ultra-understanding.

Flex your mind-muscle. A macho attitude alone won't do it. Intelligence, humour and ambition are also important.

Attention and admiration. Don't forget to admire her, desire her and pay her compliments.

Whatever you do...

- **DON'T** feel sorry for yourself.

- **DON'T** be indecisive and ask her to make all the decisions.

- **DON'T** be pessimistic and constantly worry about the future.

- **DON'T** emphasise your allergies, aversions, etc.

- **DON'T** be too obvious about your interest.

Remember, never confuse sex with romance. A physical encounter with an Aries woman doesn't mean you have stirred her deeper emotions.

- **DON'T** be too flashy in an attempt to impress her.

- **DON'T** be reluctant to have sex in unusual places.

- **DON'T** tell her that you prefer going go to bed early enough to get eight hours sleep every night.

- **DON'T** imply that women are not cut out for male professions.

- **DON'T** plan everything.

She doesn't mind entering into a casual relationship that's based only on friendship and sex.

Signs you're in - or not

If you've caught her eye, there will be plenty of signs. She will chase you, play with you, tease you – and then pull back to see if you're still interested. The challenge is to determine the depth and seriousness of her interest. She may regard you as a possible partner – or just see you as a fun lover. These are some signs that her intentions may be more serious:

Chances are she will...

- approach you and invite you out
- pay attention to the things you're interested in
- make you feel special and desired
- surprise you with fun text messages
- suggest that you join her and some friends for a weekend away
- hint at erotic interest

Not your type? Making an exit

It's unlikely that you'll ever find yourself stuck in a relationship with an Aries. She has no time for men or relationships that don't inspire her – and if you're not too keen on her, yours will qualify. She believes that life is for living and exploring – not wasting time on a clueless guy who doesn't appreciate adventure. She may be too busy to notice at first, but as soon as reality hits her, she'll be off.

There are always exceptions to this rule, although they're rare. If your Aries insists on sticking it out with you, you might need to be firmer. She will probably be confused at first, and as soon as she realises that you're serious, she'll get mad. At this point, there's no turning back.

Foolproof exit measures:

Before you try any of these, be prepared to take cover – and don't come out until she's left. They will infuriate her.

- Tell her to lose weight
- Criticise her 'tacky' underwear – no matter how delicate or classy it might be
- Act indifferent about sex and display little or no enthusiasm for it
- Flirt with other women, and pretend not to notice when she gives you the eye
- Demand that she be more submissive
- Insist on knowing everything she's up to

CHAPTER 3

SEX'N STUFF

Seductive moves:
How to get her in the mood:

She is attracted to strong men who can introduce her to new worlds of erotic pleasures, but she doesn't need you to be exotic about it. She's not into Tantric sex or the Kama Sutra. That kind of slow, careful attention to positions would drive her nuts. She has no patience for elaborate lovemaking. Something simple, juicy and a little sassy is enough to spark her interest – and her passion.

Preferences and erotic nature

Sex with an Aries woman must always be a mutual thing. If you expect her to live out her creative side, you must do your bit as well. She is ruled by energy, and her need for adventure applies to her erotic life, too. She'll tingle with excitement about anything out of the ordinary. Visuals, either still or live, can be very arousing for her. If you decide to try role playing, never opt to take the passive part. She doesn't like passive guys – even if it's just an act.

Hitting the right buttons

Although every sign has areas on the body that are more sensitive than others, individual sensitivity may vary quite a bit. Don't go body-blind. Honing in on these erogenous zones and forgetting the rest of her is not a good idea. Use these areas to create sparks while turning her on, and as a passion-booster when things get heated. Watch her body language – including the most obvious of signs. Open your mind to the sensuality of touch and taste.

Key areas
Her face, forehead, scalp and ears

Get it on
Whenever you want to whisper something to her, make sure to brush gently against her ear with your tongue or lips. Although it may not seem like much to you, this contact produces tiny tingles all over her body.

Arouse her
In addition to her ears, pay close attention to her face and scalp. Careful, light touches with your fingertips across her face can have a magic effect. Light kisses in these areas will give her goosebumps. But fair warning: don't start playing around with these erogenous zones unless you're serious about having sex. As soon as you've managed to turn her on, she'll expect you to deliver.

Surprise her
Pull her close, tell her how beautiful she is and how much you want her, gently bite her earlobe – and let her go. Turn around and start doing something completely different. It won't be long before she touches your shoulder and asks you if there's anything else on your mind…

Spice it up
Set the alarm clock a little earlier than usual and surprise her in the shower. You can also give her an exotic gift: an erotic toy, an aromatic oil or sexy underwear.

Remember: No matter how tired and uninspired you may be, never act indifferent while having sex with her. If you're not feeling up to it, it's better to let her know and save it for another time.

Her expectations

Be assertive. Be erotic. Be fun! Her preferences in bed? Easy! She likes anything that is fun, exciting and adventurous. She expects her partner to be assertive and sensual. If he can impress her with erotic creativity, she'll probably put him on speed dial.

Admiration and desire. Her partner needs to compliment her body and her lacy underwear, especially if she gives him a private striptease. She's confident in her body and enjoys showing it off. She knows exactly how to move in order to excite her partner...

Don't linger too long. Although she thinks foreplay is nice, she prefers to move on to the main course pretty quickly. Fiddling about with her erogenous zones for too long can make her restless. She wants and needs a strong partner who's able to satisfy her craving for playful and passionate sex.

Show some energy. She is an assertive sexual partner and tends to take command in bed. However, that doesn't mean her man can just lie back and enjoy it. He needs to make an effort to please her – and if he doesn't, he'll be out of her bed very quickly.

Your sensual preferences
Quiz yourself and find out whether this woman is for you.

Where on the scale are you?
1 = Don't agree | 3 = Sure | 5 = Agree!

1. If the erotic mood is right, the 'when' and 'where' don't really matter.
One a scale for 1 to 5, you are: 1 - 2 - 3- 4 - 5

2. Attention to your partner's body is important, both before and during sex.
One a scale for 1 to 5, you are: 1 - 2 - 3- 4 - 5

3. It's essential that a woman is as passionate and assertive as her man.
One a scale for 1 to 5, you are: 1 - 2 - 3- 4 - 5

4. New experiences should be the rule, not the exception – provided they feel natural and fun.
One a scale for 1 to 5, you are: 1 - 2 - 3- 4 - 5

Score.
15 - 20: This is a passionate union... If the mood is right, you'll probably try to squeeze in several erotic moments each day.
10 - 14: She probably knocked your socks off the first time you spent the night together ... and you have probably been addicted since then.
5 - 9: She may be a little too much at times, but the pleasure keeps you buzzing.
1 - 4: This could be a challenge. If you don't communicate your needs and preferences, she may run over you.

CHAPTER 4

GENERAL STUFF

The big picture

Keep in mind that the characteristics of a Aries may vary quite a bit depending on where within the sign she was born, as well as a wide range of additional astrological factors. But for now, let's stick to the basics. Just remember: don't jump to conclusions as soon as you meet her. Give her room to shine. Get to know the woman behind the sign.

Her personality: Pros and cons

Pros
- Enthusiastic
- Energetic and lively
- Efficient
- Assertive
- Intelligent, with a sharp mind
- Independent
- Confident and courageous
- Feminine and attractive
- Charming
- Adventurous
- Responsible
- Interesting and engaging
- A loyal friend
- Passionate

Cons
- Arrogant
- Cynical
- Dislikes weakness
- Snobbish
- Aggressive
- Impatient
- Ignorant
- Pushy
- Possessive
- Insensitive
- Superficial
- Romantically restless
- Vain
- Obsessed with the chase

Tip: How to show romantic interest

Romance with an Aries woman will always be based on adventure and mutual interests. Gifts, chocolate and flowers are out. Invite her along for something dynamic and fun: a rafting trip, a local wine tasting, etc.

Romantic Vibes

Miss Aries:
The energetic and inspiring partner

The essence

Why wait? She is determined when it comes to romance, and she doesn't mind taking the initiative – in fact, it's natural for her. She is very goal-oriented, so she'll never sit around and wait for a guy to make a move.

Teasing and chasing. An Aries woman can make a suitor go slightly crazy. She may clown around, be charming and attentive and make him feel like he's the most interesting man in the world – and then suddenly pull back and play hard to get. It may sound a little mean, but that's not her intention. She simply loves the chase – and the male attention.

A little bit of both... Although she may fantasise about a macho guy, deep down, she longs for a gentleman who woos her with love and loyalty.

***My* man!** If she has fallen for someone, she will approach him directly and push all female competition aside. Some men may find this overzealous, but if the guy is scared off by her assertiveness, he's not for her.

Adventurous and fun. When she finally finds her man, she will be an amazing partner. She will take the initiative to experience new things – whether an exotic holiday or simply something fun at home. The relationship will never get old. Life with the female Aries will always be an adventure.

Tip: How to show erotic interest

Be direct. Admire her body. Smile seductively and touch her gently... She is no slow starter, and she will pick up on your hints very quickly.

Erotic Vibrations

Miss Aries:
The passionate and assertive lover

The essence

Spicy erotic menu. Sex and sensuality mean a lot to her, but she doesn't need an all-nighter to feel satisfied. Sometimes a passionate and impulsive quickie is all it takes.

No prude. If the mood turns hot unexpectedly, she may be persuaded to have sex in an unusual place.

Sassy and assertive. If you are used to being in charge – and sexually, literally on top – you should prepare yourself for a surprise or two. The female Aries is an assertive woman who enjoys being in command. However, she's no erotic steamroller. She is feminine and playful.

Passion and presence rule! She is always present in the moment and engaged in her erotic feelings. Men who have experienced this woman sexually will often rate the encounter among their lifetime highlights.

No mixed signals, please. Never mislead the Aries woman. If you have given her the impression that you're ready for sex, then you'd better deliver! If you don't, she will write you off as a hopeless cause.

A sensual firework. She is a dream when it comes to bringing sparkle and adventure to your sex life. Satisfying her partner is just as important to her as her own satisfaction.

CHAPTER 5

COMPATIBILITY QUIZ

Are you banging your head against the wall, or does she unleash your positive potential? Do you provoke her or bring out the best in her? Is she making you throw your arms into the air in exasperation, or do you feel inspired and complete in her company? Take the test to find out.

Question no 1
You've been looking forward to a nice, romantic weekend at home. How do you respond when your partner tells you that she's planned to take you to an erotic exhibition and then to a show?

A - Wow! Great fun!
B - I would appreciate her initiative, but I'd ask her to take one of her friends instead.
C - That's just typical. Whenever I want a quiet weekend, she wants to take off somewhere. This woman is wearing me out!

Question no 2
When do you feel the most intense excitement?

A – When they draw the lucky numbers during the weekly lottery on TV.
B – When engaging in physical activities like skydiving, scuba diving or skiing.
C – During passionate and adventurous sex.

(cont.)

Question no 3
How well do you deal with an independent and ambitious woman?

A – Quite well, provided she's not aggressive or demanding.
B - Not very well. This whole 'independence' thing puts me off. What's wrong with a man being a man and a woman being a woman?
C – Very well. I respect women who are ambitious and achieve their goals.

Question no 4
How would you normally approach a woman you're meeting for the first time?

A – With loads of compliments, even if I don't mean half of what I'm saying.
B – With humour, intelligence and masculinity.
C – With a playful and seductive smile.

Question no 5
The two of you are out having a drink. How would you react if your girlfriend told a woman off for flirting with you?

A – It would be a little embarrassing, but it'd be nice to know that she cares.
B – I wouldn't like that. An innocent flirtation can make the day more exciting.
C – I'd love that. I think it's great when a woman is prepared to tell the world: 'That's my man; lay off!'

Question no 6
Do you ever leave your girlfriend wondering whether you want to have sex or not?

A – Yes – that's a game I love to play.
B - Never! When I feel like having sex, I playfully tell her: 'I want you! I want you now!'
C - Sometimes, but I never intend to tease her.

Question no 7
How do you feel about having a partner who is strong and passionate in bed?

A - That's all I've ever wanted!
B - I dislike dominating women. I would prefer a soft, sensitive, cuddly and romantic partner.
C - I don't mind, provided she gives me the opportunity to dominate her every now and again.

Question no 8
Are you easily aroused?

A - Sometimes. It depends on my mood.
B – Oh, yes.
C - I firmly believe that sex should be planned in advance. The setting needs to be right.

Question no 9
How would you react if your girlfriend surprised you on your birthday by filling your home with cheerful party people?

A – I'm not into surprises – especially surprise parties.
B – I don't know ... I'd have mixed feelings, but I'd probably enjoy myself.
C – Great fun!

Question no 10
On a scale from 1 to 10, how impulsive are you?

A – A solid 10. I'm so impulsive it's almost a hassle sometimes.
B - Around a 1 or 2. I find impulsiveness very distracting.
C – Somewhere in the middle. Sometimes I'm impulsive, sometimes I'm not.

SCORE	A	B	C
Question 1	10	5	1
Question 2	1	10	5
Question 3	5	1	10
Question 4	1	10	5
Question 5	5	1	10
Question 6	1	10	5
Question 7	10	1	5
Question 8	5	10	1
Question 9	1	5	10
Question 10	10	1	5

75 – 100
How does it feel to know that you've captured the woman of your dreams? You won't have many boring moments in your life – the Aries woman will see to that! Your sex life will be an adventure, too. You know exactly how to handle her, and she loves it. There is no need to discuss or justify anything. You're on the same level, and you share a basic understanding of what makes life fun and interesting. There is no need to look elsewhere. The person who can make you happiest is right by your side.

51 – 74
As long as you stick with her, you will never be bored. There might be a few passionate arguments, but the occasional thunderstorm always clears the air and leaves the earth fresh and fertile. You feel free around her and can talk to her about anything, including your intimate needs and desires. She is no prude, and she gets a kick out of your juicy ideas. She truly loves strong, intelligent men, so don't hold back on your masculinity – but don't put on a show, either. Be yourself and nurture your ambitions. Take care of this woman – she's going to bring you a lot of happiness.

26 – 50

You may feel torn between two worlds. On one hand, you love your partner's energy, enthusiasm and optimism, and the fact that there's never a challenge too big to overcome. On the other hand, you sometimes feel drained. You wish there was more structure and peace in your life. It all boils down to your feelings, values and aspirations. If you're not clear on what those are, then it might be a good idea to find out. If your love is strong and your values are shared, there ought to be a path you can follow. The worst thing you can do is close your eyes and hope for the best. When you finally open them again, she may already be gone...

10 – 25

Do you ever actually communicate, or are you just shouting at each other? Have you ever tried to understand her needs – truly? Do you feel that she's neglecting your needs, too? You are probably either too bossy or too timid for her taste. It'll take great care to make this relationship work. You'll have to make quite a few sacrifices – and is it really worth it? The female Aries is passionate, fun-loving, ambitious and impulsive – and always on the go. Deep down, you know she's an inspiration and a great source of energy. But can you handle her? And does she have what it takes to make you happy?

Thoughts...
If you don't communicate, you won't be able to set things straight. Never rush to conclusions.

TAURUS the female

YOUR DATE: TAURUS
21 April–20 May

The Essence of her

Charming – feminine – determined – wise – self-disciplined – confident and strong, but longs for a masculine man – quality-conscious, both about people and things – reliable and responsible – loyal – sensual and romantic – sensitive to atmosphere – generous and kind – genuine and honest – hard-working – realistic – down-to-earth – has a fondness for beauty

...and remember: She is friendly and open, but she won't reveal too much right away. She prefers to get to know people before she opens up.

Blind Date – speedy essentials

Who's waiting for you?
If she has to wait for you, she will probably keep looking at her watch and glancing towards the door. She'll hate to think that you've stood her up. However, if she's early and has some time to kill, she might just browse through a magazine while sipping a drink. She won't mind; she enjoys her own company. She will be stylish, feminine and attractive. You'll notice something playful in her eyes, but you'll soon discover that she's saving a lot for later. What you're getting is a preview.

Emergency fixes for embarrassing pauses.
With a Taurus woman, pauses are warning signals – and a cue for you to get your act together. She is far too polite to allow a conversation to be stuck for long. But if she starts glancing across the room, she might be thinking 'What am I doing here?' If you like her, mention something interesting or fun you've done: taken a DJ gig for a local jazz station, written a book or an article, trekked through wilderness or even just cooked something impressive ... but whatever it is, be modest about it.

Your place or mine?
If you find yourself in bed with her on the first date, then you must have made a profound impression. In fact, you must be close to her vision of the perfect guy. She seldom has casual sex – not because she's a prude, but because she doesn't get any real satisfaction from sex with a man she doesn't know. Sure, a little fun is OK, but a one-night stand is usually more hassle than anything.

Checklist, before you dash out to meet her:
Be on time
(hint: never make her doubt you)
Send a quick text beforehand, confirming the date
(hint: she appreciates the small details)
Wear a nice outfit, but nothing over the top
(hint: casual masculinity will do)
Be well groomed, but with no – or very little – cologne
(hint: keep it clean and natural)
Have some info about the menu or the place
(hint: be prepared)

Tip: She is sensual, independent, confident – and strong enough to be weak. When she finds the right man, she will allow him to become the king of her life.

CHAPTER 1

PREPARE YOURSELF

Catch her eye, capture her attention
Top 10 attention grabbers

1. Show your strong and masculine side.
2. Make sure your comments are smart and often humorous.
3. There's no need to be a free spender when you're out, but be generous.
4. A personal gift that shows you have paid attention will go a long way.
5. Give her your complete attention. No distracting glances at other women.
6. Ask her to call you to let you know that she's home safely.
7. Be stylish and elegant – no matter what you're wearing.
8. Show support and enthusiasm for her projects and ideas.
9. Be compassionate and considerate.
10. Sport a little luxury, but no bling.

The HE. The man!

The Taurus woman prefers cool cats, not kittens. You won't find her obsessing over a cute butt. She appreciates the features of a man that reflect his strength, like arms and shoulders. She respects a man's integrity and will prioritise personal qualities over looks. However, if she can, she'd like to have both.

The Essence of him
Attentive– intelligent – down-to-earth – playful, enthusiastic and creative – has a fondness for comfortable luxuries – sensitive to beautiful and sensual – has an alert mind – enjoys the arts, music and exquisite food – confident– compassionate – loyal and trustworthy – sensual and erotic – strong and fit

---

Taurus arousal meter
From 0 to 100… In an hour or two. She normally needs time to get into the mood. However, visual stimulation can speed things up considerably. Try a very innocent erotic move – no porn!

Remember: Be true to yourself
It doesn't matter if she is the most stunning girl you've ever met – if you don't match, you don't match. You may be able to put on a show for a while to hold her attention, but what's the point? We can't please everybody. We all have different needs, dreams, tastes and preferences. There's no such thing as a one-size-fits-all lover. Be yourself, and be true to who you are – always!

Very important: A cheap present will be regarded as an insult – unless there's a personal story behind it.

CHAPTER 2

THE FIRST DATE

Getting your foot in the door
The basics

No cheap hook-up lines. 'Hey babe, fancy a bit of man' is definitely not the right approach. This is a feminine, sensual, classy and romantic woman, and cheap remarks will get you nowhere. In fact, if you want to seduce her, you'll need to avoid anything cheap.

Polish your manners. The Taurus woman expects to be treated gallantly, so polish up your manners and put your best foot forward. Be attentive and polite.

Let's go out. Invite her out, but not to a place that offers juicy discounts and supersaver quarter-pound burgers. If you suggest this, she'll probably think you're joking. If you can't afford to splash out on a fancy meal, be clever about it: invite her on a picnic in a scenic place.

Be attentive. The Taurus woman loves receiving compliments and small tokens of affection: a sweet comment, a kiss on the cheek, a hug, an unexpected text or phone call, a little gift.

Never take her for granted. Make sure she feels valued, respected and appreciated.

Whatever you do...

- **DON'T** be pushy. Allow her to make up her mind.

- **DON'T** be cheap.

- **DON'T** give her any reason to doubt you. Be reliable.

- **DON'T** be careless about your appearance.

- **DON'T** show off or brag about yourself.

Remember, She can be very slow about showing her interest, and she may need a nudge once in a

- **DON'T** be too extravagant. She may start worrying about making it up to you.

- **DON'T** flirt with other women, no matter how innocently.

- **DON'T** take her attention and generosity for granted.

- **DON'T** get into petty arguments.

- **DON'T** pretend to be interested if you're not.

while. If you haven't heard from her, send her a text.

Signs you're in - or not

When courting a Taurus woman, there are two things to keep in mind: 1) she's a slow mover; 2) she's not great with hints. Be straight with her. The challenge is to deliver straightforwardness in a gentle manner. A man who suddenly declares his love after casual, friendly interactions will freak her out! However, she does appreciate persistent men – provided they are classy about it. This makes her feel desired and gives her time to make up her mind. But even when she's decided she's interested, she can be surprisingly reserved, especially considering how assertive she is in her professional life. However, if she really likes you and feels comfortable around you, she may give you a few hints:

Chances are she will...

- show genuine interest in you and pay you compliments
- give you a gift – a very nice gift
- offer to do something for you
- pamper you with attention and maybe a massage. She will call and text you
- be protective of you

Not your type? Making an exit

The Taurus woman is the most loyal woman in the zodiac. She is also extremely protective. If someone were to touch a hair on her man's head, they'd be sorry – very sorry. Like a raging bull or a fierce mama bear, she will take on anyone to protect the people she loves. Her relationships are precious, and that's why she waits a long time before committing herself to a partnership. Her loyalty is too valuable to waste on someone who's not worth it.

But sometimes, she gets too comfortable. Sometimes, she fails to see that life has more to offer, and she sticks around ... and sticks around ... and sticks around. Breaking up with her isn't easy, especially because her romantic relationships have a tendency to turn into friendships – and who would break up with a friend?

Foolproof exit measures:

If you're tired of being her buddy and miss being somebody's hot lover, there are a few options to help you move on. Some examples include the following:

- Stand her up, and offer feeble excuses for why you didn't show
- Push her into making decisions about the future
- Criticise her work ethics, her morals and her commitment
- Be demanding and ungrateful
- Be rude and inconsiderate towards others
- Criticise her friends and family
- Flirt with other women, both online and in the real world

CHAPTER 3

SEX'N STUFF

Seductive moves:
How to get her in the mood:

The Taurus woman is not particularly impulsive, so erotic surprises are not her thing. Take your time to get her in the mood. As soon as she gets going, she'll keep going. Either way, there will be no quick mood changes – unless you watch an erotic movie together. Her sex life is passionate and precious, and she shouldn't be rushed.

Preferences and erotic nature

She appreciates a real and genuine man – no fakes or wannabes. She is most easily turned on by a muscular and strong body. However, if the man has an erotic mindset and sensual personality, then his looks are less important. She loves being kissed and touched all over, as well as having seductive suggestions whispered in to her ear. She appreciates clean, natural scents. Cologne can turn her off in bed. She needs to take her time, and she expects her lover to respect that. He needs to be sensitive and assertive at the same time.

Hitting the right buttons

Although every sign has areas on the body that are more sensitive than others, individual sensitivity may vary quite a bit. Don't go body-blind. Honing in on these erogenous zones and forgetting the rest of her is not a good idea. Use these areas to create sparks while turning her on, and as a passion-booster when things get heated. Watch her body language – including the most obvious of signs. Open your mind to the sensuality of touch and taste.

Key area
Her neck and throat

Get it on
The slightest touch on her neck can send goosebumps all the way down to her toes. The move may seem innocent, but this region of her body is a very powerful 'on' button. It's a convenient erogenous zone for stimulating her both privately and in public.

Arouse her
If you have just met her, you can 'accidentally' touch her neck while helping her with her coat or giving her a goodnight kiss on her cheek. If things are getting a little more intimate, brush over the area with soft lips, gentle nibbles and light touches with the tips of your fingers. She won't be able to handle much of this before passion takes over. Be prepared.

Surprise her

Make the setting romantic. Set out candles, fresh flowers and sensual snacks that will be suitable for intimate play later – like whipped cream, strawberries and creamy chocolate sauce. Her romantic mood can turn erotic – quickly.

Spice it up

She is highly sensual, and pleasant sensations involving taste, touch and texture will please her: the softness of silk against her body, warm oil gently rubbed over her chest, or a touch of honey enjoyed off her neck ... be creative.

Remember: Never push her into trying anything she's not keen on. She will expand her erotic horizons willingly – but at her own pace.

Her expectations

The magic touch. Although the Taurus female may be described as traditional and conservative in bed, she is far from boring. She doesn't need to reinvent traditional positions; she has her own way of making them very pleasurable.

Keep it comfortable. She's not into kinky stuff, and her fantasies tend to remain fantasies. She does, however, get a kick out of having sex in different places, including outside. But she has no delusions about sex on the beach in the moonlight, with grains of sand going everywhere. For her, sex needs to be comfortable, no matter where it happens. So make sure to bring a blanket!

A little tenderness. It's important to her to receive small gestures of affection when making love, like cuddles and kisses. She is not a demanding lover, but she will expect her partner to show initiative and passion. A quick one under the covers with the lights out will offend her.

Light her fire. Sex is important to her. Her sensual pleasures are often guided by her feelings, which is why she seeks deeper connections with sexual partners.

Embrace the moment. Her lover needs to pay close attention to her needs; she expects him to be just as passionate as she is.

Your sensual preferences
Quiz yourself and find out whether this woman is for you.

Where on the scale are you?
1 = Don't agree | 3 = Sure | 5 = Agree!

1. Experiencing each other through touch and taste increases sensual pleasure.
One a scale for 1 to 5, you are : 1 - 2 - 3- 4 - 5

2. There is no such thing as passionate sex without a comfortable setting.
One a scale for 1 to 5, you are : 1 - 2 - 3- 4 - 5

3. A constant need for erotic adventures can make you superficial and restless.
One a scale for 1 to 5, you are : 1 - 2 - 3- 4 - 5

4. Romantic feelings can make sex far more intense.
One a scale for 1 to 5, you are : 1 - 2 - 3- 4 - 5

Score.
15 - 20: Steamy, intense, passionate – and loving. Enjoy!
10 - 14: She may be a slow starter at times, but as soon as her interest is sparked, she'll make up for the delay.
05 - 09: She may require a bit more passion and intensity than you're used to. Give into her sensuality and explore new erotic depths.
01 - 04: Your preferences are completely different to hers. Flexibility and communication will be important to achieve a satisfying sex life.

CHAPTER 4

GENERAL STUFF

The big picture

Keep in mind that the characteristics of a Taurus may vary quite a bit depending on where within the sign she was born, as well as a wide range of additional astrological factors. But for now, let's stick to the basics. Just remember: don't jump to conclusions as soon as you meet her. Give her room to shine. Get to know the woman behind the sign.

Her personality: Pros and cons

Pros
- Generous
- Loyal
- Friendly
- Supportive
- Determined
- Sensual and passionate
- Feminine and playful
- Humorous
- Romantic
- Productive
- Persistent
- Reliable
- Genuine
- Self-disciplined

Cons
- Lazy
- Stubborn
- Materialistic
- Overindulgent
- Slow starter
- Conservative
- Reluctant to change
- Conventional
- Narrow-minded
- Cautious
- Unimaginative
- Overly sentimental
- Unforgiving
- Afraid of failure

Tip: How to show romantic interest

Little things will get you far. Unexpected attention makes her heart sing. Text her and let her know you're thinking about her. Offer to cook dinner or give her a backrub when she's tired.

Romantic Vibes

Miss Taurus:
The loyal and romantic partner

The essence

The soft touch. Although she may come across as practical, organised and determined, her love life is completely different.

Make a move. She is used to being assertive in her professional life, which is why she prefers her man to take the initiative in her romantic life.

Masculinity and strength. A strong man makes her feel safe and supported. It's also very important that he desires her, both romantically and erotically.

Joy! She won't fill her days will exotic sex and unexpected surprises, but there will be loads of sensual pleasures, fun adventures and joy for her and her partner.

Embrace life. She believes that life is not only for living, but also for loving – and she embraces pleasures big and small. This philosophy is important to her. A man who doesn't appreciate the finer things in life will not be able to make her happy.

Tip: How to show erotic interest

Be sensual, with a warm voice and a seductive look in your eyes. Remember, she's not good with hints. Be direct but in subtle way. If she feels cornered by your passion, she'll turn away.

Erotic Vibrations

Miss Taurus:
The sensual and tender lover

The essence

Choosy. She won't throw herself at the first guy who looks in her direction. The Taurus woman is very choosy. But as soon as she has made up her mind about a man, she evolves into a goddess of sensual pleasures.

Sensual. She knows exactly how to get her lover in the mood by dressing seductively, speaking in a low, warm and sensual voice and making the surroundings as comfortable as possible.

Say yes! She has a strong sex drive. If you want to be her lover, you mustn't turn her down very often – or at all.

Keep your promises. If you have hinted at a sensual evening, the Taurus woman will play with the thought for hours and be excited when she sees you. If you end up working late, don't expect any sympathy when you finally arrive. The hot vibes will be gone. A cold shoulder is probably all you're going to get.

CHAPTER 5

COMPATIBILITY QUIZ

Are you banging your head against the wall, or does she unleash your positive potential? Do you provoke her or bring out the best in her? Is she making you throw your arms into the air in exasperation, or do you feel inspired and complete in her company? Take the test to find out.

Question 1.
Would you describe yourself as observant?

A. No. I can be extremely absentminded, and I often wander around in my own world.
B. Sometimes, if I smell a new perfume or something cooking, or anything vivid like that.
C. Yes. I pick up on hints easily.

Question 2.
Where would you prefer to have sex?

A. In a luxurious hotel room.
B. I'm not that particular. Any place is good enough for me.
C. In comfortable surroundings: a large, soft bed with soft music, candles, loads of cushions, a bottle of champagne...

(cont.)

Question 3.
When it comes to sex, what's most important?

A. Adventure and playfulness.
B. Passion and sensuality.
C. Not sure. Sex is no big deal.

Question 4.
If you were buying your partner a surprise gift, what would you go for?

A. I know she loves luxury … maybe a nice pair of shoes or a cashmere sweater.
B. I'd keep it simple. Flowers – she'd love that.
C. Presents are for birthdays and Christmas!

Question 5.
Do you compliment your woman when you're out with friends?

A. Yes, of course I do. I'm very proud of her.
B. Not really. Either I forget – or can't find a reason to compliment her.
C. Sometimes, when it feels natural.

Question 6.
Is financial security important to you?

A. Piggybanks and savings accounts are not my style.
B. Yes – financial security means financial freedom.
C. I try, but I'm not all that great with budgets and spreadsheets.

Question 7.
Do you often make an effort to please your woman – in general?

A. Every now and then – provided I've got the time and feel up to it.
B. Of course I do; I love her!
C. I seldom find time for that.

Question 8.
How would you respond if your partner told you she had splashed out on a very expensive silk nightdress?

A. I would have told her off for being financially reckless. That's crazy!
B. Well, it's her money. She can do whatever she wants with it.
C. I enjoy having a seductive woman lying next to me in bed...

Question 9.
Do you expect your partner to play along every time you're in the mood?

A. No. Sometimes we're busy with other things and not focused on sex. It's normal.
B. Of course. When I want sex, I want it now!
C. Not really – even though I wish she would.

Question 10.
Do you think it's OK to enjoy weekend-type- treats – wine, special food, etc. – during the week?

A. No. It's important to distinguish between weekdays and the weekend.
B. Yes, of course. Every day is for living – not just Friday, Saturday and Sunday.
C. Sure, provided I can afford it.

SCORE	A	B	C
Question 1	1	5	10
Question 2	5	1	10
Question 3	5	10	1
Question 4	10	5	1
Question 5	10	1	5
Question 6	1	10	5
Question 7	5	10	1
Question 8	1	5	10
Question 9	10	1	5
Question 10	1	10	5

75 – 100
You probably feel like you've found the woman! She is strong, positive and confident, and she keeps your spirits high, no matter what happens. She wakes you up in the morning with a gentle kiss and a playful sparkle in her eyes. Your friends are probably envious. Keep treating her like a princess, and she'll do her best to live up to your expectations. Sometimes people just click. Why overthink it? Just enjoy and cherish it.

51 – 74
Life is wonderful. You have found a woman who satisfies and inspires you. Sure, you'll have a few heated discussions. But although you don't always agree, you respect each other's opinion. You are probably a little more sexually assertive than she is, but this could actually be an advantage for her – provided you don't push her. Pay careful attention to her moods. As you probably know, this woman doesn't wear her heart on her sleeve. When in doubt, ask her. And don't settle for a 'Oh, it's nothing'. If you communicate well, you will avoid silly misunderstandings. And one final note: Don't forget to compliment her whenever she has made an effort to please you.

26 – 50
Every now and then, you may wonder whether it's worth it. But if you really love her, you should give it a try. Barrelling forward with your fingers crossed won't do the trick. You'll need to make a concerted effort to understand each other. Is she acting slightly boring? This could be her way of showing you that she's unhappy with how things are. The worst you can do in a situation like this is to nag her. Yes, she can be stubborn. Although this may provoke you, try guiding her instead of pushing. You will be surprised to discover how much you can achieve if you approach conflicts with humour rather than anger. Show her your charming, sensual and tolerant self, and watch how she brightens up!

10 – 25
You might as well face it: this won't last long. A romantic relationship should be based on love, not practical arrangements. It may be time for both of you to explore the mysteries of love – elsewhere. You deserve something better, and so does she.

Suggestion

A quiz may give you a few hints, but life offers amazing and sometimes surprising nuances. If you make each other happy, then embrace the joy, cherish the love and explore the opportunities ahead!

GEMINI the female

YOUR DATE: GEMINI
21 May–20 June

The Essence of her

Impulsive – a quick decision-maker – charming – lively – inventive – likeable – enjoys making things happen – loves luxury in all facets of life – sensually intuitive – assertive – a good multitasker – outgoing and loves socialising – optimistic – a free spirit – influential – positive and constructive – open-minded

...and remember: She is always on the move, either in her mind or out in the world. New experiences feed her energy and enthusiasm for life.

Blind Date – speedy essentials

Who's waiting for you?
She will be smiling and probably wearing something eye-catching; wonderful colours, a bold design or unique accessories. She will be eager to meet you and buzzing with energy. If you're late, she will probably be talking with somebody already. She enjoys people and is very sociable. Whatever shyness she may feel initially will disappear as soon as the two of you start talking. She will radiate enthusiasm and positivity – provided her date isn't holding back and being too serious.

Emergency fixes for embarrassing pauses.
If you manage to make her sit in silence, you will have either utterly dazzled her with your looks and charm or turned her off completely. If you make a lousy impression, she won't stay long. On the other hand, if she really likes you, you can loosen her up with fun stories, innocent gossip and interesting facts. It won't take long before she's back to her sparkling self.

Your place or mine?
Whichever is the most convenient. The Gemini woman loves adventure and may easily be seduced into having sex on a first date. However, you'll need to be careful. If you really like her but fail to satisfy her in bed, she won't return your call the next day. She needs her man to be on the same level as she is, both mentally and physically. Merely a quick burst of passion will probably turn her off.

Checklist, before you dash out to meet her:
Have a few interesting facts or stories ready
(hint: Entertain her)
Wear a stylish outfit and a few expensive accessories
(hint: Be classy)
Make reservations at a nice place
(hint: She loves luxury)
Have some creative ideas, like getting a massage at a spa
(hint: Pamper her)
Be well-groomed, minding your face hands and hair
(hint: No scruffiness)

Tip: Never underestimate her. Although she may demonstrate a naïve femininity, she's very smart. If you fail to appreciate this, she will probably move on quickly.

CHAPTER 1

PREPARE YOURSELF

Catch her eye, capture her attention
Top 10 attention grabbers

1. Wear a stylish outfit and maintain an aura of masculinity.
2. Show her your charming personality.
3. Exhibit a confident and friendly attitude towards people around you.
4. Demonstrate generosity and pamper her.
5. Make intelligent comments and ask interesting questions.
6. Wear a big smile.
7. The Gemini woman will appreciate assertiveness and taking the initiative to try something new.
8. Exude playful boyishness, while keeping your feet on the ground.
9. Show off a luxury item, like a stylish car.
10. Be impulsive – surprise her.

The HE. The man!

The Gemini woman wants a little bit of everything. Her man needs to be strong, masculine and caring, but not possessive or restrictive of her freedom. He must be adventurous and free-spirited, but never make her feel insecure. He must be playful and energetic, but still responsible and reasonable. It's a tall order, and all about finding the right balance.

The Essence of him
Flexible in his views – tolerant – liberal and open-minded – strong and masculine, but not too body-focused – good-looking and well-dressed – adventurous – creative in bed – playful and enthusiastic – entertaining in social setting – protective and caring – generous – with a fondness for the good things in life – intelligent– optimistic – has a good sense of humour

---

Gemini arousal meter
From 0 to 100... In 10 minutes, provided you have managed to spark her imagination, or responded to an erotic suggestion with enthusiasm.

Remember: Be true to yourself
It doesn't matter if she is the most stunning girl you've ever met – if you don't match, you don't match. You may be able to put on a show for a while to hold her attention, but what's the point? We can't please everybody. We all have different needs, dreams, tastes and preferences. There's no such thing as a one-size-fits-all lover. Be yourself, and be true to who you are – always!

Very important: If you ask for her opinion, make sure to pay attention. If you come back with the same problem the next day, she will look at you strangely and wonder why you didn't get the point the first time.

CHAPTER 2

THE FIRST DATE

Getting your foot in the door
The basics

Excite and inspire. She needs new experiences to thrive. Men who fail to inspire her won't stand a chance. She may be charming and polite for a while, but it won't last. Hold onto her attention by being interesting.

Ask for her advice. She is a keen listener and will always give you her opinion.

Engage and fascinate. Brush up on your knowledge about all sorts of things: culture, politics and even gossip. People born under this sign enjoy a bit of gossip.

A luxury... Take her out to an expensive restaurant. She loves luxury and her conversation flows naturally over a glass of champagne. Don't be a cheapskate! Giving her a gift? Try something unusual. When in doubt, a luxurious item by a famous brand will usually be a hit.

Don't hold back. She loves intellectual and active people. Show your adventurous, dynamic, spontaneous and exciting sides – well, maybe not all at the same time...

Whatever you do...

- **DON'T** ask her to split the bill.

- **DON'T** come on too strong.

- **DON'T** choose the cheapest items on the menu.

- **DON'T** forget to compliment her ideas.

- **DON'T** talk about boring everyday topics.

Remember, she expects you to be just as energetic and impulsive as she is. Don't get lazy and

- **DON'T** forget your manners and start knocking back food and drink.

- **DON'T** underestimate her by asking silly questions.

- **DON'T** be pessimistic.

- **DON'T** criticise her opinions or tell her to face reality.

- **DON'T** be too absorbed in yourself and your own views.

make her take the lead. Everything needs to be mutual, or she will lose interest.

Signs you're in - or not

If she likes you, she will show it. She seldom waits for the guy to make the first move. Her philosophy is: If you want something, go for it! Why waste precious time just staring at the phone and hoping he will call? She'd much rather get a 'no' than keep wondering. And deep down, she doesn't expect you to say no! Her intuition is good, and she usually has a feel for whether a guy is interested or not. If you're not sure about her intentions, look for these signals:

Chances are she will...

- be the first to call and text after a date, and she will always text you back right away
- invite you to an exhibition, a special party or something similar
- get you a gift based on something you've talked about
- make room in her life to see you frequently
- take an interest in your interest
- share her sensual thoughts and ideas...

Not your type? Making an exit

Getting out of a relationship with a Gemini woman is easy – very easy. She is a free spirit, always on the move and searching for inspiration, ideas and adventures. She needs a man who can keep up with her and preferably lead the way from time to time. She sees life as too precious to be wasted on boring relationships. She needs energy and excitement, and craves a man who is dynamic and spontaneous. Her life is for living – and loving someone who shares her values.

If things aren't working out, she will probably be the first to go. She has a very low tolerance for miserable situations. However, if she has fallen for you completely, or if she's too busy to notice that you're no longer fascinated by her, it will be up to you to wake her up to reality.

Foolproof exit measures:

Make sure you really want to break up with her before you go ahead these measures – because when she's gone, she's gone.

- Stop taking her seriously and begin to question her ideas
- Take her camping and sleep in a dirty tent
- Reduce sex to a once-a-week, under-the-covers event
- Criticize her for spending money on pointless luxury
- Be selfish, and start sulking and complaining about everything
- Act indifferent about your looks, including the way you dress

CHAPTER 3

SEX'N STUFF

Seductive moves:
How to get her in the mood:

The Gemini woman is impulsive, flexible and tolerant, and turning her on – or at least sparking her erotic interest – is quite easy. But don't take her sexual interest for granted. If she suspects you're only looking for a quick one before going to sleep, she will probably suggest making you a mug herbal tea instead. This woman is no sleep aid.

Preferences and erotic nature

She loves men with a taste for adventure – including in the bedroom. New, erotic suggestions excite her. As a playful lover, she appreciates anything that can make her sex life more exciting, including sex toys. Don't be surprised if she suddenly pulls out a couple of interesting-looking, vibrating items. A man who can expand her horizons without being too kinky makes her tingle . He must be creative and respect her assertiveness and need for change – including her sensual suggestions. A traditional man-on-top guy won't remain in her bedroom for long. Foreplay is also important to a Gemini woman. And if her partner uses his creativity when touching her, she will respond with increasing passion...

Hitting the right buttons

Although every sign has areas on the body that are more sensitive than others, individual sensitivity may vary quite a bit. Don't go body-blind. Honing in on these erogenous zones and forgetting the rest of her is not a good idea. Use these areas to create sparks while turning her on, and as a passion-booster when things get heated. Watch her body language – including the most obvious of signs. Open your mind to the sensuality of touch and taste.

Key areas
Her arms, palms and fingers

Get it on
If you were to accidentally brush your fingers over her hands, you might notice a slight flush to her cheeks. The slightest touch to her hands, palms or lower arms might trigger an intimate reaction.

Arouse her
Focus on her hands and fingers. One of the advantages of her erogenous zones is that you can arouse her anywhere you like, without people noticing. However, if you want to move onto the real stuff, you may want to start in the comfort of a private place. This woman simply loves having her hands and fingers sucked, licked, kissed and even bitten. Use your imagination.

Surprise her
Give her a gentle hand massage. Make sure to use lots of cream or oil to allow your hands to slide easily over, and between, her fingers. Finish off by gently caressing her with the tips of your fingers...

Spice it up
Playing erotic games can actually be quite fun – but don't make them too complicated. It will be important not to allow the planning to take the fun and impulsiveness out of it.

Remember: She may have been chasing you, but if you fail to live up to her expectations, she will leave as quickly as she came.

Her expectations

No rush. The Gemini woman's preferences can be summed up very succinctly: She likes anything that is exciting and adventurous – provided you don't rush her into it.

Be prepared. Sex with her is not confined to the bedroom. She's up for having sex in all sorts of unusual places. If the mood arises while the two of you are out driving, she may respond positively to having sex in the backseat of your car – depending on where you are, obviously.

Active and assertive. She is assertive and enjoys being sexually active. Never suggest that she should play more passive role. That will turn her off.

Keep it fun. She usually gets more pleasure from fun and exciting sex than intensely passionate sex. ' Hot and steamy', to her, means a sticky gym.

Try something new. She may suggest having sex simply because she is looking for a new adventure. She'll satisfy her need to explore while you'll get excitement with added erotic pleasure: a win-win situation.

Attentive. No matter what her preferences might be, she will always try hard to please her partner. Very few men will feel disappointed after a night with this amazing woman.

Your sensual preferences
Quiz yourself and find out whether this woman is for you.

Where on the scale are you?
1 = Don't agree | 3 = Sure | 5 = Agree!

1. Playfulness and new ideas are the key to a happy sex life.
One a scale for 1 to 5, you are: 1 - 2 - 3- 4 - 5

2. Sex should never be confined to a certain place or time.
One a scale for 1 to 5, you are: 1 - 2 - 3- 4 - 5

3. A creative and assertive sex partner brings out the passion in me.
One a scale for 1 to 5, you are: 1 - 2 - 3- 4 - 5

4. Impulsiveness is important in order to live out your sensual feelings.
One a scale for 1 to 5, you are: 1 - 2 - 3- 4 - 5

Score.
15 - 20: You both appreciate impulsiveness, adventure and playfulness. This could be fun.
10 - 14: This woman will keep you on your toes, and you like that. Your erotic life will be sparkling.
05 - 09: Her impulsiveness can be a challenge at times, but it may also broaden your erotic horizon.
01 - 04: Does she have a bit too much energy at times? If you cherish quiet, sensual moments, this could be a challenge.

CHAPTER 4

GENERAL STUFF

The big picture

Keep in mind that the characteristics of a Gemini may vary quite a bit depending on where within the sign she was born, as well as a wide range of additional astrological factors. But for now, let's stick to the basics. Just remember: don't jump to conclusions as soon as you meet her. Give her room to shine. Get to know the woman behind the sign.

Her personality: Pros and cons

Pros
- Creative
- Energetic
- Adventurous
- Charming and feminine
- Clever
- Open-minded
- Sociable and friendly
- Sexually intuitive
- A good listener
- A lover of people
- Playful and enthusiastic
- Attractive
- Assertive in bed
- Liberated

Cons
- Restless
- Prone to gossip
- Impatient
- Needs to be liked
- Uses her looks to her advantage
- Maintains shallow relationships
- Superficial
- Has low stamina
- Romantically indecisive
- Antsy
- Fakes luxury with bling
- Hyperactive
- Ignores her own feelings
- Emotionally distant

Tip: How to show romantic interest

Be generous and even a little old-fashioned. She's not one for subtle hints. Flowers, gifts and lots of attention will do the trick ... pamper her and let her know you want to spend more time with her.

Romantic Vibes

Miss Gemini:
The positive and energetic partner

The essence

Embrace life! Life is an adventure, and she embraces every opportunity to explore something new in any part of her life, including in her relationships. She doesn't want a life filled with boring routines. This may be part of the reason that Gemini women often have quite a few relationships before settling down.

Commitment doesn't scare her. She actually looks forward to it. The challenge is finding the right man, someone who shares her enthusiasm for adventure.

Find the right balance. Security is important to her, but too much makes her restless.

A jewel. She is attractive and feminine and will always shine when she's out with her man. She gets a kick out of making him proud.

Enthusiastic. She's interested in all sorts of things and easily becomes inspired to try something new. There's seldom a dull moment in her life.

Emotional space. A little bit of everything. Activity and energy are at the core of her character. Too many romantic evenings at home can make her antsy.

Tip: How to show erotic interest

Easy. All you have to do is make a suggestion. Make it playful and interesting, and avoid being blunt or crude. Be seductive about it. Use your voice and your eyes.

Erotic Vibrations

Miss Gemini:
The playful and creative lover

The essence

Keep it exciting. Don't expect her to be satisfied with missionary position or settle for sex once a week in a dark bedroom. Hold onto her interest by being creative.

A little research... If you're not feeling particularly creative in the sex department, do a little research. Don't introduce anything new unless you know what you are doing. Bringing a textbook to bed will turn her off. A few nice visuals, on the other hand – well, that's a different matter...

Don't rush it. She won't respond well to being pushed. Allow her to set her own pace.

Tune in. Make sure your sensual antennas are perfectly tuned. Her mood can change from super hot to ice cold in two seconds if you fail to interpret her wishes correctly.

A sensual butterfly. Her need for change can sometimes result in her moving from one partner to another – but this will only happen if she's in a casual relationship.

Broaden your horizons. Don't be put off if you get the impression that she's trying to adjust your ways in order to make your sex life more interesting. This can actually be very rewarding and broaden your sexual horizons.

CHAPTER 5

COMPATIBILITY QUIZ

Are you banging your head against the wall, or does she unleash your positive potential? Do you provoke her or bring out the best in her? Is she making you throw your arms into the air in exasperation, or do you feel inspired and complete in her company? Take the test to find out.

Question 1.
Your girlfriend has been giving you erotic hints all evening. How do you react when she suddenly forgets about the whole thing?

A. I don't like that at all. You should finish what you've started – no matter what.
B. No big deal. We'll make up for it soon anyway.
C. It can be a little frustrating, but her impulsiveness is part of what makes her so attractive.

Question 2.
Your girlfriend has surprised you by booking a weekend away for the two of you, attending a fun seminar. How do you respond?

A. This is one of the things I really love about her: she makes life so interesting and exciting.
B. Without asking me about my plans? Inconsiderate.
C. I prefer to plan things myself, but sometimes I do need a kick in the butt.

(cont.)

Question 3.
What does a relaxing weekend look like to you?

A. Sitting in front of the fireplace reading a book.
B. Doing odd jobs around the house during the day; going out and having fun in the evening.
C. Taking off somewhere to experience something new and exciting.

Question 4.
Do you think it's important to try out different things to keep your sex life interesting?

A. I don't want to get stuck in a routine, but I'm not fanatic about trying new things.
B. You only live once. My life, including my sex life, should be exciting.
C. No. I'm not all that into sex. I prefer closeness and tenderness.

Question 5.
Do you mind if your girlfriend has male friends?

A. Not at all. Why should I?
B. It depends on whether I know who they are.
C. Yes. What's wrong with our mutual friends?

Question 6.
How do you feel about a girl who seems more interested in an exciting sex life than tenderness and sensuality?

A. That's fine by me.
B. Not my style at all. I prefer warm and sensual women.
C. I think it's important to have an exciting sex life, but it's equally important to experience intimacy during sex.

Question 7.
Do you regard yourself as creative?

A. Creative? Where's the dictionary?
B. I wouldn't necessarily describe myself as creative, but I've got a vivid imagination.
C. Yes, absolutely.

Question 8.
Do you find it boring to take turns pleasing each other?

A. That depends on my mood. Sometimes, I prefer to just get straight to the point.
B. Not at all; I love it. It gives me a chance to enjoy my partner.
C. Yes. How boring can you get?

Question 9.
How do you feel about independent and professional women?

A. I support traditional gender roles: a man should be a man, and a woman should be by his side.
B. I'm really cool with successful women, provided I still get to feel like a man.
C. No problem at all. I support equal opportunities in every aspect of life.

Question 10.
Are you able to express sexual feelings verbally?

A. Yes! I often whisper naughty nothings into my girlfriend's ear.
B. Verbal sexuality? Is this something new?
C. Yes, but only if I'm in the mood.

SCORE	A	B	C
Question 1	1	10	5
Question 2	10	1	5
Question 3	1	5	10
Question 4	5	10	1
Question 5	10	5	1
Question 6	10	1	5
Question 7	1	5	10
Question 8	5	10	1
Question 9	1	5	10
Question 10	10	1	5

75 – 100

Running out of ideas? Never! Wish there were more hours in the day? Probably! For the two of you, every day is a new adventure waiting to be explored. You seize the moment and embrace every excitement that comes your way. Impulsiveness is at the core of your relationship, and that makes it fun and unpredictable. You will never be bored. The two of you are perfectly matched, no doubt about it. No advice needed. You know exactly how to handle your woman.

51 – 74

Fun and excitement are a major part of your life. Who cares if it can get slightly hectic? You're having a great time. The only thing to watch out for is that you don't start trying new things just for the sake of it. This could make you feel shallow and restless. Make sure to devote time to your deeper feelings, both romantic and sexual. But you've already mastered the joy, adventure and freedom that are the key to her heart; it comes naturally to you and everything seems to be running smoothly. No big issues. No major discussions. Wonderful days ahead.

26 – 50

It may feel like you're stuck at a crossroads. There are several options, but you cannot make up your mind. You long for more depth and stability in your life, but you are also attracted to the impulsiveness and adventure the Gemini woman brings. Still, it can be difficult to keep up with her at times. She's always juggling several tasks at once, whereas you prefer to keep a singular focus. Sometimes you wish she could be a little more thorough, and you know she often wishes she could spur you into action. Both of these are possible. Happiness is within reach. Just be careful not to sacrifice your own needs to fulfill hers. A relationship should be a place for growth, not a battleground.

10 – 25

Why are you holding onto a relationship that gives you so much grief? Chances are, if you don't do anything about it, she will. If your feelings for her are strong, talk to her before it's too late. There are solutions to everything, and you can make it work – if you want to. Life is too short to waste on arguments and disappointments. It's time to be true to yourself and to each other. Your need for comfort, closeness and stability might be impossible to establish with her – but you'll have to talk to her to find out.

Thoughts...
Sometimes, a challenge is what we need in order to grow. However, only accept a challenge for the right reasons. Make sure your heart is in it. Love should be real. Never pretend.

CANCER the female

YOUR DATE: CANCER
21 June–22 July

The Essence of her

Sensitive – incurably romantic – generous with her time and compassion – loyal– attractive, with a flair for turning every outfit into something stunning – appreciates the beauty in life – dramatic – moody – charming – sensual and seductive – playful – practical – affectionate – kind and considerate

...and remember: She may come across as strong and independent, but she has a sensitive nature and is easily hurt. Mind your words and be careful with criticism. Diplomacy is the key.

Blind Date – speedy essentials

Who's waiting for you?
She would rather not wait for you, but she'll give a bit of slack – provided you have a very good excuse for being late. She is a woman in every sense of the word, and she exudes femininity. You'll see it in her outfit, her make-up, the way she carries herself, her sparkling laugh and the way she looks at you... A Cancer woman won't be shy. Being around men energises her. She is used to male attention, and she expects to be admired. Her standards are high. If you don't meet her expectations, she will be polite and have dinner with you – but that's it. She'll be off and you'll be out.

Emergency fixes for embarrassing pauses.
If you feel a pause coming on, it's your cue to get your act together. She will happily chirp along with a man who fascinates her, but she doesn't like being bored. If the conversation comes to a halt, it's your job to pick it up. Don't try the 'you-look-beautiful-tonight' routine. She already knows – don't patronise her. Focus on ideas or dreams – topics that make her think and connect with you.

Your place or mine?
Either. Ideally, she would like to be whisked away by a prince on a white horse, but this is the 21st century, and she's flexible. She'll probably be open to a fling for one of two reasons: first, if she hopes the guy will turn out to be something worthwhile – or second, if he's stunning and probably good in bed. In either case, he needs to meet her expectations. He must be attractive, manly and attentive.

Checklist, before you dash out to meet her:
Going to a new place? Get directions ahead of time
(hint: don't spend forever trying to find the place)
Be groomed and pay attention to details!
(hint: nails, nose hairs... she'll notice)
Wear something stylish and clean
(hint: don't just throw something on at the last minute)
Be rested and energised
(hint: no yawning!)
Prepare some topics for conversation
(hint: keep her entertained)

Tip: The Cancer woman is generous, compassionate and kind – provided you don't rub her the wrong way. Her tolerance for criticism is very low. Keep it positive.

CHAPTER 1

PREPARE YOURSELF

Catch her eye, capture her attention
Top 10 attention grabbers

1. Be polite: take her coat, open the door etc.
2. Have a confident and relaxed attitude in public.
3. Wear something stylish you stand out.
4. Focus exclusively on her – don't allow for any female competition.
5. Notice something unique about her – even a small detail – and compliment her on it.
6. Be assertive! Show your interest, but without being blunt about it.
7. Portray yourself as masculine and protective.
8. Surprise her: hire a limo for an hour and go sightseeing, or take her on a mini-trip.
9. Add a little extra luxury to a date.
10. Walk up to her with a single flower, and hand it to her even before you speak.

The HE. The man!

Although she's independent and strong, she's looking for a man who can protect her and take care of her. He needs to be someone she can admire and be proud of. Loyalty is very important to her, and her partner must never give her reason to doubt him. She values little gifts and dinner invitations not for the gifts themselves, but for the gestures. They're tokens of love, and she cherishes them.

The Essence of him
Diplomatic – able to handle her various moods – handsome and stylish – generous– attentive – understanding – strong and masculine, without being blunt or macho – romantic – sensitive to the finer things in life –loyal, supportive and faithful –entertaining in social settings – engaging – inclusive

Cancer arousal meter
From 0 to 100... In an hour or a week, depending on how well she knows you – or whether she's really attracted to you. If she's got the hots for you, it may be less than an hour!

Remember: Be true to yourself

It doesn't matter if she is the most stunning girl you've ever met – if you don't match, you don't match. You may be able to put on a show for a while to hold her attention, but what's the point? We can't please everybody. We all have different needs, dreams, tastes and preferences. There's no such thing as a one-size-fits-all lover. Be yourself, and be true to who you are – always!

Very important: Although she can be a great flirt, she's choosy about the men she invites into her life for the longer term. The first impression counts.

CHAPTER 2

THE FIRST DATE

**Getting your foot in the door
The basics**

No silly remarks. You need to be careful when trying to seduce this woman, as she is one of the most sensitive signs in the zodiac. A stupid remark at the wrong time could ruin the entire evening – and the possibility of a romantic encounter with her!

Don't take anything for granted. She has high standards, but she's not a difficult woman to handle – far from it! She is sympathetic and understanding, and she'll go to great lengths to sort things out with her partner. However, until you capture her heart, you'd better play your cards right!

Be romantic and sensitive. Try an intimate evening in small restaurant with soft music in the background.

Be attentive, both when you're together and when you're not. Notice any changes in her appearance, and after the date, call or text to let her know you're thinking about her.

Be generous. Flowers never go out of fashion with Cancer women. Be generous with your time, as well. Take an extended lunch break to see her, or finish your workday early.

Whatever you do...

- **DON'T** neglect your manners, especially at the table.

- **DON'T** take her for granted. Show appreciation and affection.

- **DON'T** be crude or use bad language.

- **DON'T** try to entertain her with lame jokes or silly stories.

- **DON'T** pinch her bum!

Remember, although you have captured her interest, she'll be quick to turn her back on you if you mess up. Always keep your word!

- **DON'T** tell her the restaurant is 'just fine' if she doesn't like it.

- **DON'T** criticise her friends or family.

- **DON'T** be blunt about your erotic feelings.

- **DON'T** suggest skipping dessert or going for low-calorie items on the menu.

- **DON'T** be sloppy about your appearance.

Be classy, attentive, charming – and someone she can admire. There are no second chances with this girl.

Signs you're in - or not

The Cancer woman enjoys being around men. She flirts and teases – and loves the attention. This is where things can get a little tricky. She may shoot you seductive glances and dazzle you with her charm and laughter, but it doesn't mean she's necessarily attracted to you. Sometimes, male attention is all she's looking for: she expects to get it, and she always does. A man who ignores her will be written off as a nutcase. If she really likes you, there are some signals that may give her away:

Chances are she will...

- buy you a gift – something small but exclusive
- take the initiative to call or text you
- be available on short notice when you ask her out – even during the day
- keep her focus firmly on you when you're out in public
- make hints about the future: an idea about a weekend away together, etc.
- open up and tell you about her preferences – in all areas of her life

Not your type? Making an exit

The Cancer woman has a romantic vision of what a relationship should be. She thinks life would be wonderful if it was like an old-fashioned romance novel. When reality catches up with her, she tries to be practical about it. Although she can be surprisingly realistic, she has a deep longing for love and romance – and she's prepared to endure quite a bit, provided her partner is worth it. If she finds herself in an unhappy relationship, she may prefer to try loads of different things rather than putting her foot down and leave.

If she's not ready to let you go, she will do whatever she can to hold onto you. She will use tears and dramatics. If that doesn't work, get ready for a guilt trip. And her last resort...? Putting up a fight. Breaking up with a female Cancer is no easy task. You'll save yourself a pile of trouble if you can let the initiative come from her.

Foolproof exit measures:

You'll need to make sure you are ready to take these steps, because they'll make you look really bad – and before they work, they will rock the boat more than you thought possible.

- Criticise her when she has made an effort to please you
- Give her a cheap gift picked up from the local petrol station
- Compare her to other women and suggest that she change
- Be quick and selfish in bed
- Suggest having pizza and streaming porn on your date night
- Criticise her opinions and argue over details

CHAPTER 3

SEX'N STUFF

Seductive moves:
How to get her in the mood:

Don't be fooled into thinking you know how to get her going. You may – or you may not. What she needs depends on her mood. Sometimes, she's receptive. Other times, you might as well try to seduce a rock. But no matter how you go about it, remember to be smooth and sensual. If you come on too strong too suddenly, you won't have a chance.

Preferences and erotic nature

She's not an exhibitionist, but she would probably enjoy slowly undressing in front of you. If she does, remember to compliment her body. This will make her even more eager to please you. Sex and romance are two sides of the same coin for a female Cancer, so romantic gestures often arouse her. You'll notice this when you whisper sweet nothings into her ear, gently stroke her hair or give her a tender kiss. These moves can make her knees go weak. But if you carry on caressing her body, you'd better prepare for a long and sensual night.

Hitting the right buttons

Although every sign has areas on the body that are more sensitive than others, individual sensitivity may vary quite a bit. Don't go body-blind. Honing in on these erogenous zones and forgetting the rest of her is not a good idea. Use these areas to create sparks while turning her on, and as a passion-booster when things get heated. Watch her body language – including the most obvious of signs. Open your mind to the sensuality of touch and taste.

Key area
Her chest

Get it on
Take a good look at the female Cancer. Chances are that she's well equipped in the chest area, and this is a good place to focus if you want to bring out the passion in her. This may sound easy, but it's not. Grabbing a boob will probably result in a smack on the head. Your touch needs to be gentle, almost accidental – at least in the beginning...

Arouse her
If you want to arouse her in public, you'll need some finesse. She hates vulgarity, so be subtle. If you're out dancing, let your upper body gently brush against hers. When helping her with her coat, let your hand brush against her breasts. When you're in bed, well ... that's up to you. Be warm, loving and gentle, and you can't go wrong!

Surprise her
Although she is naturally romantic and sensual, she's also moody. Springing something on her if she's not ready will annoy her. If you want to surprise her, make it gradual. Make dinner while she relaxes with a refreshment, let her know a romantic idea you have, give her a sensual backrub – though preferably after dinner, otherwise the food might get cold...!

Spice it up
Use an item that you wouldn't usually bring to bed – something that will stimulate her senses: a warm and aromatic oil, a piece of cashmere to caress her body or a little whipped cream ... keep it sensual.

Remember: She may come across as a kitten, but she is passionate in bed. Her erotic repertoire is impressive, which is the result of her creativity – and her experience.

Her expectations

Sweet suggestions. Don't even think about suggesting anything vulgar; it could put her off sex for weeks. Suggesting a bonk in the copy room at work will seldom go over well (unless, you've really managed to dazzle her).

Sensual setting. When focusing on seducing her, it's important to pay attention to the setting. The female Cancer usually prefers to have sex in the comfort of her own, or her partner's, home. Set the scene with candles, soft music, a glass of wine … the works.

Keep the lights on. When it comes to the bedroom, she enjoys caressing and fondling her partner's private parts. Don't turn off the lights, because she enjoys admiring them as well.

Frisky and feminine. Although she's not particularly shy, she's rarely sexually aggressive. She may give the man some hints, but she usually prefers him to take control.

Strength and sensuality. She wants a passionate, caring and gentle partner. Touches and caresses should always be soft.

Your sensual preferences
Quiz yourself and find out whether this woman is for you.

Where on the scale are you?
1 = Don't agree | 3 = Sure | 5 = Agree!

1. Caresses and sensual touches are important during sex.
One a scale for 1 to 5, you are: 1 - 2 - 3- 4 - 5

2. Sexual gadgets can be fun, but they're not necessary if the relationship is satisfying.
One a scale for 1 to 5, you are: 1 - 2 - 3- 4 - 5

3. Intimacy and closeness are the basis for a rewarding sex life.
One a scale for 1 to 5, you are: 1 - 2 - 3- 4 - 5

4. Patience is important in the bedroom. Rushing things can ruin the mood.
One a scale for 1 to 5, you are: 1 - 2 - 3- 4 - 5

Score.
15 - 20: Your connection is intense, romantic and very sensual. Enjoy this erotic dream.
10 - 14: The Cancer woman can occasionally be shy. Be patient, guide her gently and let her ease into things.
5 - 9: You probably wish she could be a little less sensitive at times, but it's her nature. Take your time. Enjoy her sensuality.
1 - 4: Either she's too sensitive, or you're too impatient – but you could both benefit from expanding your erotic horizons together.

CHAPTER 4

GENERAL STUFF

The big picture

Keep in mind that the characteristics of a Cancer may vary quite a bit depending on where within the sign she was born, as well as a wide range of additional astrological factors. But for now, let's stick to the basics. Just remember: don't jump to conclusions as soon as you meet her. Give her room to shine. Get to know the woman behind the sign.

Her personality: Pros and cons

Pros
- Kind
- Generous
- Thoughtful and considerate
- Romantic
- Warm and caring
- Soft and feminine
- Attractive
- Affectionate
- Charming and entertaining
- Smart
- Sparkling
- Has an eye for beauty
- Idealistic
- Practical and efficient

Cons
- Sharp-tongued
- Moody
- Overly sensitive
- Possessive
- Prone to overindulgence
- Argumentative
- Self-pitying
- Demanding
- High-maintenance
- Emotional
- Has no tolerance for criticism
- Insensitive when provoked
- Self-obsessed
- A drama queen

Tip: How to show romantic interest

Show romantic attention the old-fashioned way. Try texts, calls, flowers, gifts, dinner invitations ... it's all fair game! Make her feel special, but make sure not to overdo it. If you crowd her, she will probably take off.

Romantic Vibes

Miss Cancer:
The romantic and attentive partner

The essence

Either you're in - or not! As soon as she has entered into a relationship, she'll consider you a serious couple. Liberated do-as-you-please partnerships are not her style. If a man feels the need to nurture his free spirit, as far as she's concerned, he can free his spirit somewhere else. She is prepared to make an effort in a relationship, provided her partner shares her enthusiasm.

Romance is everything. Even though she may have short-lived relationships, she seldom refers to them as flings or 'a bit of fun'. Instead, she regards them as little romances. Although she may enjoy a physical fling, love is the fundament that keeps her trying.

Show appreciation. A man will always feel proud to have a Cancer woman by her side. But if she makes an effort to socialise and help him out in social settings, she'll expect him to appreciate her for it later.

Precious attention. Small tokens of affection can make her intensely happy: a loving text message, a rose for no reason, an unexpected gift or some help with something she finds boring. However, when it comes to birthdays or other occasions, she'll expect a nice gift, so you'd better splash out. Something small and sweet will result in an icy stare.

Tip: How to show erotic interest

She can read men like most people read the newspaper. If you're in the mood, a seductive look is usually all it takes to let her know. Add a charming smile, and then look away and allow your interest to sink in.

Erotic Vibrations

Miss Cancer:
The tender and affectionate lover

The essence

Seductress. Although she's undeniably feminine, this woman is no sensitive flower. She can be quite the seductress if she's in the mood – or if she's met a man who dazzles her.

Direct, but subtle. She will never throw herself at a man. She prefers to create sensual sparks by shooting him flirtatious glances. She'll expect him to take it from there. Her hints are gentle, but they're always very direct. A man who doesn't get the message is probably in a coma.

Getting into it. She needs time to loosen up, so don't be impatient. As soon as you have got her in the right mood, she'll prove to be an energetic and engaged lover.

Romantic-erotic flavours. She has the unique ability to combine passion, sensuality and romance: a cocktail that can intoxicate most men. When she finds her man, she will be completely focused on him. The intensity will either scare him off or make him feel like a stud.

In the mood, or moody. She needs to feel intimately and sensually connected to her partner. Don't try seducing her when she's got her mind on other things – or when *you* do. Trying to persuade her to have sex when she's not in the mood will usually end in bad feelings.

CHAPTER 5

COMPATIBILITY QUIZ

Are you banging your head against the wall, or does she unleash your positive potential? Do you provoke her or bring out the best in her? Is she making you throw your arms into the air in exasperation, or do you feel inspired and complete in her company? Take the test to find out.

Question no 1
Do you always tell your woman about your erotic fantasies?

A - Yes, of course I do.
B - My woman is very sensitive, and I try to avoid things that might upset her.
C - Sometimes, but only when I feel they're important to express.

Question no 2
You've been looking forward to a hot and steamy evening. How would you react if your girlfriend lit candles and put on some soft music?

A - I'd love that. I love easing into sensual moods ... it makes everything more intense.
B - Typical. Whenever I want a passionate night, she turns into a soft, cuddly and boring little thing.
C – I might be a little disappointed at first – but I'd be confident that she'd please me by the end of it...

(cont.)

Question no 3
Are you sensitive to your partner's needs?

A - I try, but sometimes I forget – and sometimes, I don't know what she expects from me.
B - Yes. That's very important when you're in a relationship.
C - Only if it will benefit me somehow.

Question no 4
How would you feel if your partner started to sulk after a minor upset?

A – I'd feel annoyed and tell her to pull herself together.
B – I'd leave her alone and give her space until she felt better.
C – I'd talk to her and try to understand her feelings.

Question no 5
How often do you make use of previous experiences with your partner when having sex?

A - I always recall what has previously made my girlfriend happy, and then I build on it.
B - Sometimes I do, sometimes I don't. It depends on the mood.
C - Not really. I usually try to do something new.

Question no 6
You have finally decided to throw out the old jumper you were wearing the first time you met your girlfriend. How would you react when you found it back in your wardrobe the next morning?

A - I'd smile, shrug and leave it there.
B - I'd ask my girlfriend to choose a new jumper for me so we can get rid of this one.
C – I'd throw it away – again!

Question no 7
Do you find it easy to talk about your feelings or any emotional issues?

A – It can be difficult, but I'm willing to try – if I must.
B – Why do feelings have to be involved in every little thing? I hate this 'let's talk' stuff.
C – Yes, I don't have any problems with that.

Question no 8
Be honest: do you enjoy flirting with women other than your partner?

A – Of course. That's what all guys do.
B - I enjoy the attention, but I would never do anything to upset my partner.
C – No, not just for the sake of it. I'm just friendly – with everybody.

Question no 9
Would you say you enjoy the good things in life?

A – Yes: I love good food, a nice atmosphere, close friends and a loving girlfriend...
B – Yes, I enjoy hiking and sleeping outside in my tent. Nice to wake up with the birds.
C – Yes: a fancy car, a nice flat and luxurious holidays are important to me.

Question no 10
Which of the following is an example of something you'd do to please your partner?

A – I'd fix her car or washing machine or something.
B – I'd surprise her with a little gift or a bunch of flowers.
C – I'd take an interest in what she's doing, either her work or hobbies.

SCORE	A	B	C
Question 1	1	10	5
Question 2	10	1	5
Question 3	5	10	1
Question 4	1	5	10
Question 5	10	1	5
Question 6	10	5	1
Question 7	5	1	10
Question 8	1	5	10
Question 9	10	1	5
Question 10	1	10	5

75 – 100
Somehow you know it's right ... it just feels good. Your woman loves your strength and attentiveness, and you embrace her softness, warmth and femininity. You're like two jigsaw pieces, a perfect fit. You are different, but you still seem to match. You're a team, both moving in the same direction. You communicate very well and are sensitive to each other's needs. No silly misunderstandings or upsets here – everything flows effortlessly. This is very promising. Keep inspiring each other...

51 – 74
Apart from a few minor conflicts, this is a pleasant and happy relationship. Togetherness is important to both of you – not only physically, but also mentally. Being on the same level and supporting each other makes everything run smoothly. There's no need to discuss erotic preferences – sensuality is the driving force for both of you. She may be a bit stubborn at times, but remember that there's usually a reason that she puts her foot down – even if you don't agree. She is very sentimental and likes to hold onto what's familiar to her. Don't push her into something new overnight; it will only make her feel uneasy.

26 – 50

'If only she could be a little more [fill in the blank]...' If this comment ever pops up in your mind, it's time to rethink the relationship. You'll either need to accept her as she is or go looking for someone else. An element of adjustment is required for any relationship, but major changes are seldom a good sign. Maybe she feels the same way about you, wishing you would change your ways. Are you prepared to do so? If the distance between you isn't too far, go ahead and figure things out. Try to understand her. Be open and forthcoming. Agree to disagree, and don't freak out about it. If you're both prepared to give a little more of yourselves, this could turn out to be a nice relationship.

10 – 25

Are you smitten with her feminine body and the attention she gives you? Are you captivated by the way she makes you feel like a man? Well, there must be something that keeps you around, because the two of you are very different. It's possible that this relationship is based on a dream. Before you go moving into your castle in the sky – which will probably end in hitting the ground with a bang – you should figure out what you really want. You may discover that the only thing you're good at as a couple is getting on each other's nerves. Save yourself some trouble and be honest with yourself and your partner. Anything is possible, but a harmonious relationship will demand careful attention and hard work.

Thoughts...
If you are too focused on what's visible on the surface, you won't discover love's hidden treasures.

LEO the female

YOUR DATE: LEO
23 July–22 August

The Essence of her

Confident – determined – optimistic– enthusiastic, with a flair for drama – assertive and strong – temperamental – generous – restless – attractive and particular about her looks – motivational and inspirational, both privately and at work – sensual and passionate – assertive – sets high standards for herself and others

...and remember: Although she will probably approach you with friendly enthusiasm, it's up to you to hold her interest. She is genuine about everything and won't stick around just to be polite.

Blind Date – speedy essentials

Who's waiting for you?
She won't be waiting for you! This queen doesn't sit around waiting for a guy – unless he has called and told her that he'll be late, has a very good excuse and has ordered a bottle of champagne to her table. Otherwise, you'll need to be there early, waiting for her. You'll notice her immediately. She doesn't walk through a door; she makes an entrance. There's something about her that makes people look. She's graceful and sensual, and she moves with confidence. Her beauty radiates from within. She will greet you with a cheerful smile and devastating eye contact.

Emergency fixes for embarrassing pauses.
Although she's naturally bubbly, confident and outgoing, the conversation may need a slight boost before you're completely comfortable in each other's company – or if she's so dazzled by your charm and personality that she's speechless. Compliment her for something you can talk more about. Voice: Are you a singer? Movement: Are you into dancing? Get creative about it.

Your place or mine?
Preferably a luxurious hotel room... The Leo woman loves adventure and excitement. If you're handsome, attentive, charming and generous, then she may be open to an erotic encounter. She believes that life is for living, and she is no prude. But this doesn't mean she'll accept any erotic invitation. She is choosy, and her standards are high. However, the right man may just persuade her to share a few sensual pleasures...

Checklist, before you dash out to meet her:
Have a small surprise arranged: Champagne at the table, for example (hint: Be generous)
Wear clothing that emphasises your best features (hint: Avoid being too obvious)
Be up-to-date on the social scene
(hint: Suggestions going to a show or an exhibition)
Scan the news for positive stories ahead of time
(hint: No negative vibes)
Be perfectly groomed with a slight hint of cologne
(hint: Be attractive and masculine)

Tip: In her world, there can never be too much of a good thing. The more, the better. This applies to everything, from praise and sensual attention to adventure and luxury.

CHAPTER 1

PREPARE YOURSELF

Catch her eye, capture her attention
Top 10 attention grabbers

1. No matter what looks you were born with, be stunning – it's all about confidence.
2. Surprise her with something unusual.
3. Be generous but don't be a show-off.
4. Be humorous and make her laugh.
5. Approach everyday topics from a positive and constructive angle.
6. Be classy and stylish. Pay careful attention to your attire.
7. Got an expensive car or luxury item? Make sure she sees it.
8. Take her to a place where people know you and give you little extras.
9. Share something interesting you know about music, food or drink.
10. Carry yourself with style and be someone she feels proud of being seen with.

The HE. The man!

Although the Leo woman is a great flirt, she won't chase a man. She will simply draw attention to herself and wait for him to make a move. However, if he waits too long, she may already be off. Her ideal man is confident, masculine and able to sweep her off her feet. He will be attentive, handsome and generous. It's important that he gives her room to shine – and never makes her stand in his shadow!

The Essence of him
Stylish and distinguished – gallant – generous with money, affection and praise – handsome – successful, in one way or another – attentive – strong – courageous – passionate and erotic – has a flair for luxury and comfort – confident and charming around women, but never flirtatious and always loyal – physically active and fit

Leo arousal meter
From 0 to 100... In an hour – or a week. It depends on her partner. She can't be bothered to spend time on someone who fails to inspire and excite her.

Remember: Be true to yourself
It doesn't matter if she is the most stunning girl you've ever met – if you don't match, you don't match. You may be able to put on a show for a while to hold her attention, but what's the point? We can't please everybody. We all have different needs, dreams, tastes and preferences. There's no such thing as a one-size-fits-all lover. Be yourself, and be true to who you are – always!

Very important: Never compete with her for a space in the spotlight. Allow her to take centre stage, and be proud of her.

//

CHAPTER 2

THE FIRST DATE

Getting your foot in the door
The basics

Admiration is king. You will get absolutely nowhere without praise and admiration. But this won't be a problem. As soon as you meet her, you'll find yourself paying her one compliment after another without even thinking about it.

In demand. Prepare yourself for competition. This sparkling and glamorous woman has many admirers. If you want to win her over, you'd better be attentive.

Keep it positive. Don't expect her to take on your problems. She's not all that keen on problems. Her attitude toward life is optimistic, and problems rarely exist in her world – she sees challenges as temporarily setbacks. Pessimistic or over-burdened guys won't stand a chance.

Roll out the red carpet. She loves to be where the action is, so it might be a good idea to take her to a new club, a premiere at the theatre or even on a weekend abroad.

Splash out. Don't invite her out to just any old restaurant. Make it somewhere special or exclusive. Being extravagant is fine. In fact, the Leo woman will love it.

Whatever you do...

- **DON'T** flirt with other women.

- **DON'T** forget to call or text her.

- **DON'T** bother her with worries and problems.

- **DON'T** be a cheapskate.

- **DON'T** make her have to work to earn your admiration.

Remember,
Never keep her waiting. If she has shown interest in you, she expects to hear from you right away. If it seems like you're dragging your feet,

- **DON'T** ask her to split the restaurant bill or suggest she pay the tip.

- **DON'T** criticise her – not even constructive criticism.

- **DON'T** patronise her.

- **DON'T** bargain with the waiter to get a free dessert.

- **DON'T** demand her attention and talk about yourself.

she'll probably decide that you're not her type after all and move on to one of the more energetic and attentive guys on her list.

Signs you're in - or not

The Leo woman prefers being chased. But this doesn't mean she won't make an effort to show interest. If she likes you, she will let you know – and subtle hints are not her style. Her motto is 'If you want something, go for it!' The man who has managed to capture her interest will represent a challenge and an adventure for her. If she hasn't made it obvious already, these behaviours will indicate that she sees you more than a just a fling:

Chances are she will...

- show you off to her friends
- let you steal her spotlight
- treat you to something nice, like a gift or a meal
- act seductive and erotically assertive
- take the initiative to ask you out
- she will send you flirtatious texts

Not your type? Making an exit

The Leo woman loves life. She loves men. She loves attention, admiration and desire. It's very unlikely that she'll ever be stuck in a joyless relationship. She is not some feeble woman who needs a strong man by her side. She embraces every day with enthusiasm and joy. If you find yourself stuck in a relationship with a Leo, then you really must be a stunner! There must be a very special reason why she's not prepared to let go.

You won't really have to make an effort to break it off. A simple comment like 'You're pretty good in bed, but you need to kick it up a notch in order to make it onto my "top ten lovers" list' will cause her to freak out. She may lose her temper, but she won't get emotional. She's not prepared to waste emotional energy on a man she regards as a jerk.

Foolproof exit measures:

If you want to make absolutely sure that your parting-ways message gets through, try the following:

- Criticise her hot passion in bed
- Tell her to lose weight and exercise more
- Flirt with other women when you're out together
- Insist on taking control in bed – and get it over with pretty quickly
- Surprise her with a weekend away – at a cheap motel in a neighbouring town
- Focus on yourself: your looks, your job, your future

CHAPTER 3

SEX'N STUFF

Seductive moves:
How to get her in the mood:

A Leo lady wants a masculine man. She wants a guy who knows what he's doing and where he's going. Boyish playfulness can be fun, but it's not what she's after in the long run. Assertiveness is the driving force of her life, and she brings it into the bedroom as well. Her partner needs to be strong enough to appreciate her passion and even take it a bit further.

Preferences and erotic nature

She is not shy. She loves physical attention on every inch of her body. The tip of your tongue, soft and relaxed lips, the tips of your fingers ... use your imagination. Take your time. Don't confine yourself to her neck and chest; move all the way from her toes up to her thighs and tummy, and she will wriggle with pleasure. She loves showing off her body, both in bed and turning you on before you get there. Role-play can be very arousing for her – she'd enjoy meeting a strong man who reluctantly allows her to dominate him, or a more sexually insecure man who needs a confident partner.

Hitting the right buttons

Although every sign has areas on the body that are more sensitive than others, individual sensitivity may vary quite a bit. Don't go body-blind. Honing in on these erogenous zones and forgetting the rest of her is not a good idea. Use these areas to create sparks while turning her on, and as a passion-booster when things get heated. Watch her body language – including the most obvious of signs. Open your mind to the sensuality of touch and taste.

Key area
Her back

Get it on
'Are you tired, babe? Let me give you a backrub.' A slightly dated and worn-out suggestion, perhaps? It may be, but it still works well with the female Leo if you want to create a few sparks.

Arouse her
Every gentle touch to a Leo's back sends sensual signals to her brain. Your hands are not the only tools you can use to stimulate her. Try your lips, tongue and other body parts. Increase the intensity as you go along, but don't start off too rough. Pay attention to her back when you're out in public as well. Soft caresses will make her burst with anticipation...

Surprise her
Initiate sex when she least expects it. Invite her home for a long lunch – and don't tell her that it could be a very erotic lunch. Make sure to pick the right day. The interlude won't be a success if she's got deadlines or a meeting to prepare for.

Spice it up
Ask her to strip for you. Get the music going and get comfortable. Make sure to get into it – not just excited, but also vocal and suggestive. Fire her up.

Remember: Her enjoyment of taking the initiative doesn't mean you can just lie back and enjoy it all. She wants a passionate and active lover, not merely a toolbox to fiddle around with.

Her expectations

No quickies. The setting needs to be right. If you're hoping for quick one in the backseat of your car, you will be disappointed.

Know your stuff. The Leo woman enjoys being sexually assertive, but she also doesn't mind a dominating partner – provided he knows how to please her.

Body talk. Admiration plays an important role in her erotic life. She prefers to make love with the lights on, and the reason is obvious: She wants her partner to admire her body. She may even rub herself with oil during foreplay in order to make her body appear sexier.

Take your time. Don't rush her. Never move on from one thing to the next too quickly. This will annoy her. She loves taking her time and enjoying every sensation.

Exposure. She prefers positions that allow her to expose her body as much as possible, so her partner has ample opportunity to caress her and tell her how wonderful she looks.

Getting pampered. If you're tired or don't feel particularly inspired, she will gladly run the show – as long as you admire her and respond with passion.

Your sensual preferences
Quiz yourself and find out whether this woman is for you.

Where on the scale are you?
1 = Don't agree | 3 = Sure | 5 = Agree!

1. Expressiveness is liberating, and it's important for fully enjoying sex.
One a scale for 1 to 5, you are: 1 - 2 - 3- 4 - 5

2. An assertive and passionate lover is very arousing.
One a scale for 1 to 5, you are: 1 - 2 - 3- 4 - 5

3. During sex, being able to watch is almost as important as being able to touch
One a scale for 1 to 5, you are: 1 - 2 - 3- 4 - 5

4. There's no such thing as sex without passion.
One a scale for 1 to 5, you are: 1 - 2 - 3- 4 - 5

Score.
15 - 20: There's only one thing to say: Close the windows and enjoy!
10 - 14: Her passionate side may surprise you, but she won't disappoint you – far from it. She may even open a few doors to new erotic adventures.
05 - 09: Don't be put off by her assertiveness. Allow yourself to relax and let her guide the way. Settle into the erotic feelings and notice how the passion builds.
01 - 04: She might be a bit too much to handle at times. Communicate is very important. She is no mind reader.

CHAPTER 4

GENERAL STUFF

The big picture

Keep in mind that the characteristics of a Leo may vary quite a bit depending on where within the sign she was born, as well as a wide range of additional astrological factors. But for now, let's stick to the basics. Just remember: don't jump to conclusions as soon as you meet her. Give her room to shine. Get to know the woman behind the sign.

Her personality: Pros and cons

Pros
- Positive
- Generous
- Passionate
- Optimistic and cheerful
- Spontaneous and exciting
- Affectionate and loyal
- Confident
- Has a strong personality
- Attractive
- Sensual and erotic
- Assertive
- Motivating
- Genuine
- Courageous

Cons
- Self-centered
- Superficial
- Temperamental
- Jealous
- Hides from difficulties
- Thoughtless
- Ruthless
- Spoiled
- Vain
- Easily bored
- A drama queen
- Hyperactive
- Reckless
- Suppresses disappointments

Tip: How to show romantic interest

Don't hold back – on anything! Shower her with attention, but without being pushy. Pamper her with invitations and little gifts. A note on flowers: Avoid the selection at your local petrol station. Make it classy and special.

Romantic Vibes

Miss Leo:
The intense and enthusiastic partner

The essence

Keep her interested. She falls in and out of love frequently, and it takes a very special man to capture her heart.

Be attentive. Affection, attention and loads of praise are important for keeping her interest alive.

Don't get too comfortable. Never take her love for granted. A miserable Leo won't stay miserable for long, and she'll go find a more attentive male.

Telling you straight. She has a fierce temper and won't hesitate to tell you how she feels if you have upset her.

Excitement is important. This applies to her romantic life as well. She will never allow love to become a chore or even a routine. She sees love as a living thing, and she will nourish it.

Seize the moment. She doesn't get sentimental. She prefers to live her life and not spend in brooding over the past. Ex-boyfriends are ex-boyfriends.

It takes two! Although she's a warm and supportive partner, she expects her man to do his part in order to make the relationship happy and fulfilling.

Tip: How to show erotic interest

Compliment her curves, the way she moves and the sensuality that exudes from her. Tell her that she really excites you. She adores attentive men.

Erotic Vibrations

Miss Leo:
The assertive and passionate lover

The essence

Privileged. Self-confidence is her middle name, and you will seldom hear her thanking her lucky stars for providing her with such a wonderful lover. In her opinion, it's he who should be grateful!

Attractive. She never works very hard to capture a man, simply because she doesn't have to. Men are captivated by her positive attitude.

Wonderful. Although slightly self-centered, she is a fantastic lover. She can be very passionate and expressive when things get steamy.

Loosen up. A slightly reserved partner doesn't need to worry. Passionate sex with a Leo woman is usually enough to make him lose his inhibition.

Royal treatment. Her attitude about sex is very relaxed, which is part of the reason why so many men find her irresistible. She will never give her partner performance anxiety. The way she arouses him will make him feel like a king and inspire him to do his best to please her.

Make an effort. She expects her lover to make an effort in every way: he must please her physically and mentally, as well as try to look good and emphasise his masculinity.

CHAPTER 5

COMPATIBILITY QUIZ

Are you banging your head against the wall, or does she unleash your positive potential? Do you provoke her or bring out the best in her? Is she making you throw your arms into the air in exasperation, or do you feel inspired and complete in her company? Take the test to find out.

Question 1.
How would you respond if your partner told you about her previous erotic experiences?

A. Smile seductively and suggest jumping into bed...
B. I'd feel excited, but also a little worried about not living up to her expectations.
C. I'd take it with a grain of salt. Some women are all talk.

Question 2.
In a relationship, do you often flatter your partner's body?

A. Yes, whenever she deserves it.
B. Very seldom. Flattery can make a woman conceited.
C. Yes, of course I do. Everybody enjoys a bit of praise.

(cont.)

Question 3.
As soon as you arrive at a party, your partner takes centre stage and dazzles everyone in the room. How do you feel about that?

A. It's typical, and it embarrasses me.
B. I love the positive attention she attracts to herself.
C. It's OK, provided she doesn't overdo it.

Question 4.
How would you feel about a woman who has very high expectations of her partner as a lover?

A. It sounds like a fun challenge.
B. I don't really know. I wouldn't want to feel obliged to perform in a certain way.
C. Well, if that was the case, then I'd better not disappoint her.

Question 5.
What would you do if your girlfriend became overly enthusiastic about all of her ideas?

A. I would support her and make sure she kept in touch with reality.
B. I'd ask her to think about things a little more – even though she hates it when I try to temper her enthusiasm.
C. Nothing. She never listens anyway.

Question 6.
Do you think it's important to let your partner know during sex that you are happy with her as a lover?

A. Of course it is. I tell her all the time.
B. When I'm having sex, I'm having sex – why bring conversation into it?
C. Sometimes I do; sometimes I forget.

Question 7.
Do you enjoy an assertive woman who takes the initiative?

A. I don't know about that. Pushy women don't really appeal to me.
B. Yes, I'm quite assertive myself, and I need a strong and independent partner.
C. Sure, that's nice, provided she doesn't insist on running my life.

Question 8.
How important is passion in your life?

A. Passion is overrated. I prefer to take things slow.
B. About average. If you apply passion to everything you do, life can get hectic.
C. Passion is very important to me. It inspires me and drives me onwards.

Question 9.
Do you pay attention to your partner's entire body during sex?

A. No. When I'm aroused, I seldom have time for that.
B. Yes – it heightens the pleasure for both of us.
C. Yes, during foreplay.

Question 10.
How do you feel about spending money and enjoying the good things in life?

A. Pampering and giving little luxuries keep things exciting and pleasant.
B. My mottos are 'The best things in life are free' and 'Always save for a rainy day'.
C. It's important to treat each other to nice things once in a while.

SCORE	A	B	C
Question 1	10	5	1
Question 2	5	1	10
Question 3	1	10	5
Question 4	5	1	10
Question 5	10	5	1
Question 6	10	1	5
Question 7	1	10	5
Question 8	1	5	10
Question 9	1	10	5
Question 10	10	1	5

75 – 100
A fantasy, a fairy tale? Not for you two! This is real – and very rewarding. People may accuse you of draping yourselves in dreams, but you both know that dreaming is important. Dreams inspire you and bring sunshine into your lives. This relationship will be filled with positivity, enthusiasm and a fair bit of passion. Your communication is strong, and you understand each other. This applies to your intimate life as well. You know how to make the most of your sex life – and how to appreciate it. Keep enjoying life and each other!

51 – 74
She may strike you as a little too much at times, but that's probably what you need. She nudges you when you slow down and energises you when days are grey. Indifference to life is not an option for this girl. She finds the positivity in everything. She believes that life should be fun and filled with love, joy, luxury and fun opportunities. It's impossible to be annoyed with her for long. She can always make you smile, and that makes it easy to forgive and forget. Her standards are very high, and this may present a challenge if you're not particular about your appearance. Remember, she needs a man she can be proud of 24 hours a day, not only in social settings. Cherish her, and enjoy the happiness – and passion – she brings to your life.

26 – 50

Either you don't communicate, or you disagree on the most fundamental issues. Try to identify your differences in order to avoid misunderstandings. There are things you need to keep in mind if you're going to make things work: Never, ever, step on her ego. Avoid criticism; guide her and make suggestions instead. Keep yourself well-groomed – including for your intimate moments. A scruffy lover is a turn-off. Do you measure up to her standards? If not, you'd better do something about it quickly – if you want to, that is. Think about it ... is she a little too demanding for your tastes? Yes, she's fun and energetic – but is that enough to make you happy?

10 – 25

Stop criticising her. Fuss and negativity will cause her to lose her passion. Face it: if you want her in your life, you'll have to put up with her extravagant and hyper-positive personality. Are you fed up with constant demands for praise? Does money seem to be flying around? Are you secretly longing for a more stable and down to earth partner? If you want to stay in the fast lane, you'll need to speed up. But maybe it's time to take a more scenic route.

Thoughts...
Too much of anything is too much, and it's up to you to draw the line. Keep in mind that your definition might change over time. What's too much energy today, may be perfect tomorrow. Think twice before making a decision.

VIRGO the female

YOUR DATE: VIRGO
23 August – 22 September

The Essence of her

Naturally charming – choosy – high expectations – loyal to her friends and family – thorough and detailed – modest – supportive – independent – sensible and down to earth – attractive – determined – feminine and sparkling – tends to worry about details – practical – analytical – childish curiosity – sets high standards for herself and people around her – health conscious – strict work ethics

...and remember: She may strike you as strong and independent, but the essence of her has a modest streak. Deep down she is looking for a man who can protect her and keep her safe.

Blind Date – speedy essentials

Who's waiting for you?
She should NOT be waiting for you. You must be there when she arrives. The fact that you've managed to get her to go on a blind date with you, is a quite a feat. Don't mess it up by being late. This is a real woman, something you'll notice right away. She is charming, feminine and slightly reserved. But there is something about her you cannot figure out... She seems independent and strong, but at the same time modest and sensitive. That's the essence of her. She can handle world by herself, but she'd rather have a man by her side to help and protect her. But she's choosy...

Emergency fixes for embarrassing pauses.
Don't despair if the conversation slows down a little. She has a modest streak and can get a little sky. Gently guide the conversation onto something positive and safe – avoid the latest stupidity from the political scene. Show interest in her and what she's doing, without being inquisitive. Make her feel relaxed in your company.

Your place or mine?
Neither. Sex on a first date is not an option. For her to let go of her inhibitions and give in to erotic feelings, she needs to feel completely relaxed. To be relaxed with someone she doesn't know – on a first date – is not easy. You may charm her, but that doesn't mean she is sexually attracted to you. In her opinion, dropping the clothes on a first date is a bit tacky and her style.

Checklist, before you dash out to meet her:

Clean shirt, polished shoes, nice haircut
(hint: Be tidy)
No heavy cologne or other smells
(hint: Her tolerance is low)
Cell phone on silent
(hint: Focus on her)
Hungry, but not starving
(hint: Enjoy your food, slowly)
Up to date on interesting topics
(hint: Appeal to her mind)

Tip: You cannot fake your way to her heart or bed. She won't let you into her life before she knows and trusts you. A fling with her is not very likely.

CHAPTER 1

PREPARE YOURSELF

**Catch her eye, capture her attention
Top 10 attention grabbers**

1. Be stylish, masculine and polite.
2. Warm voice and gentle eyes.
3. Be completely focused on her. Forget the other women in the room.
4. In a restaurant, know your stuff (food and wine), but don't be a show-off.
5. Show consideration for others. Let her know you have a big heart.
6. Pay attention to your hands... make sure they look good.
7. Make the conversation relaxed and entertaining.
8. Keep it humorous and make her laugh.
9. Pay attention to details and behave like a gentleman.
10. Be generous without splashing money around.

The HE. The man!

Her dream partner doesn't fuss about sex, he doesn't interrupt her when she's busy – and he knows there is a time and place for everything. He's also very practical and able to fix things. A dreamy poet who's unable to change a light bulb, is not her kind of man. If he's smart, ambitious and good in the kitchen – and leaves it spotless after cooking – she will start paying attention…

The Essence of him
Practical – fit and healthy – down to earth – manly, without being overly masculine – organized in all areas of life – generous, without wasting his money – creative and able to introduce her to new adventures in life – reliable, and provides her with security – stylish with a sense of quality – interesting and intelligent – good sense of humour – positive outlook on life.

Virgo arousal meter
From 0 to 100… In an hour – if she knows you and feels comfortable around you. The passion needs to build gradually.

Remember: Be true to yourself

It doesn't matter if she is the most stunning girl you've ever met – if you don't match, you don't match. You may be able to put on a show for a while to hold her attention, but what's the point? We can't please everybody. We all have different needs, dreams, tastes and preferences. There's no such thing as a one-size-fits-all lover. Be yourself, and be true to who you are – always!

Very important: Be attentive to detail. Make sure your appearance is spotless, your manners are flawless and the evening is priceless – without spending too much money.

CHAPTER 2

THE FIRST DATE

Getting your foot in the door
The basics

Measure up. There is no such thing as an easy access to this woman's heart or bed. In order to win her you need to measure up to her standards and expectations.

Appeal to her mind. In order to succeed, you need to appeal to her intellect. Her head, not her feelings, rule her heart.

Be worth while, fun, be interesting. A smart guy with a sense of humour gets her attention.

Be strong. Being able to convey strength is a good thing. Deep down she wants a man who can protect her. Her ideal man makes her relax and stop worrying. He will tell her "Don't worry, it will be all right" - and make her believe it.

Make it classy. Invite her out, but not to a noisy restaurant. She prefers intimacy. Try a quiet and romantic little bistro.

No free spending. Don't waste your money on an expensive meal. She hates to see people throw money around.

Be patient. Never rush her into making a decision.

Whatever you do...

- **DON'T** show up in a dirty shirt. She spots a spot easily.

- **DON'T** drink too much or fork down your food.

- **DON'T** be loud and tell silly jokes.

- **DON'T** be late – never keep her waiting.

- **DON'T** throw your money around to impress her.

Remember, show interest but take it slow. Be persistent without being pushy.

- **DON'T** rush her into making a decision.

- **DON'T** come on too strong.

- **DON'T** expect her to be erotically interested in you right away.

- **DON'T** forget your manners. She will notice…

- **DON'T** bring up sex and erotic topics.

Be stylish without being flashy. Be masculine without being macho. Be genuine.

Signs you're in - or not

It can be a little tricky to figure out if you have managed to do more than just spark her interest. Even though she may feel quite enthusiastic about you, she will seldom show it right away. She needs to digest the impulses and think about it. She never hurries these things, but she won't delay it either. She is practical and aware that if she doesn't make a move, some other woman will. Keep in mind she has a modest streak, which can make it a little difficult to interpret her hints. However, there are signs she is eager to spend more time with you:

Chances are she will...

- text or call you back right away
- ask you to help her with something
- ask for your opinion
- mention an activity or an event, and make subtle hints...
- offer to help you with a practical task (organizing etc)
- take time off to see you and introduce you to her friends

Not your type? Making an exit

The Virgo female doesn't move from one relationship to the other, nor give in to love easily. When she has finally found someone she is willing to commit to, she will strive hard to make things work. Although she gets emotionally attached to her partner, her life is run by reason. She would rather spend life on her own than in a destructive relationship. She does snap when her partner is not living up to her standards, but mostly because she wants to help him.

Leaving her could be easy, or it could be a little tricky. It all depends on how long you've been together. The older the relationship, the more difficult it gets. 'Forgive and forget' becomes easier as time goes by – providing you're not driving her nuts and she's about to say ENOUGH! However, if she holds on to you and her vision of love, you may want to be blunt about it.

Foolproof exit measures:

Although she is calm and down to earth, she does get hurt and upset. You need be absolutely sure before moving on with these measures.

- Make a mess, everywhere. Stop cleaning up after you
- Skip the laundry. Put on dirty shirts and sweaters
- Waste money. Tell her you're thinking about taking up gambling
- Insist on having sex all hours of the day, especially when she's busy
- Start complaining about politics, the weather, the lot
- Never be on time for dates or dinners

CHAPTER 3

SEX'N STUFF

Seductive moves:
How to get her in the mood:

The inner voice keeps messing things up. She really wants to let her hair down, but the good girl says no. That's why you may experience her eyes saying yes, but her voice saying no. A little confusing, but with the right encouragement you can make her feel naughty – and feel good about it.

Preferences and erotic nature

This may sound a little weird, but she's actually turned on by a man who knows how to fix things and handle domestic housework. Being good in the kitchen is a great plus. A sexy guy doing housework triggers her far more than other women in the zodiac.

A sudden funny and erotic comment can take her by surprise and make her think. If she's in the right mood, this will act as a self-starter. As soon as you have got her going, she will probably start smiling mischievously. She may give the impression of being proper, but with the right encouragement, you'll discover she's got a dirty mind...

Hitting the right buttons

Although every sign has areas on the body that are more sensitive than others, individual sensitivity may vary quite a bit. Don't go body-blind. Honing in on these erogenous zones and forgetting the rest of her is not a good idea. Use these areas to create sparks while turning her on, and as a passion-booster when things get heated. Watch her body language – including the most obvious of signs. Open your mind to the sensuality of touch and taste.

Key areas
Her stomach and waist

Get it on
Never make funny remarks about her tummy because this is one of her most sensitive areas - both mentally and physically. You can provoke all sorts of reactions by touching her stomach. Remember, and this is very important: NEVER touch her in such a way that she may think you're implying she has gained weight.

Arouse her
Be playful and seductive and you won't have to wait long for a positive reaction. It is very important that your touches are gentle and delicate, otherwise you risk turning her off. Suggest taking a shower or bath together. This will give you lots of opportunities to play with her erogenous zone. A casual massage is another option. Start with the back, and finish with the tummy. If you do it right, this could move on to something more sensual.

Surprise her
She's not really into surprises when it comes to sex, but a nice setting can get her going – providing she's not busy. Soft music, candles, warm oil and tasty snacks can make her relax and tune into your mood...

Spice it up
Try to experiment with oils, creams and perhaps even honey. Keep in mind, she can be a little inhibited at first, so take it slow.

Remember: She doesn't have an erotic on-button. She needs to be tuned in and turned up – not turned on. This requires patience, but it's worth it.

Her expectations

Make it sensual. She prefers lovemaking to be calm, close and sensual - with no passionate outbursts!

Make it comfortable. A dimly lit bedroom makes her feel comfortable. Forget about mirrors. This will only make her feel self-conscious and ruin the mood.

A little romance is fine... She will never overdo anything. A candle and a bottle of wine by the bedside is more than enough.

Turn on the shower... She enjoys foreplay in the bathroom. She loves the sensation of your wet body rubbing against hers. Besides, it's nice to freshen up a little before having sex... Don't take it the wrong way, just enjoy her sensual hands gently caressing you with a soft, foaming soap all over.

No acrobatics, please. In bed, she feels comfortable with the traditional positions. However, if you have something different in mind, tell her. She will probably try it - providing it it's not vulgar. If you really want to make her happy, be gentle!

Your sensual preferences
Quiz yourself and find out whether this woman is for you.

Where on the scale are you?
1 = Don't agree | 3 = Sure | 5 = Agree!

Question 1
Casual sex is too superficial to give any real enjoyment.
One a scale for 1 to 5, you are: 1 - 2 - 3- 4 - 5

Question 2
Comfortable surroundings and a nice setting is important.
One a scale for 1 to 5, you are: 1 - 2 - 3- 4 - 5

Question 3
Having sex when your mind is busy is not a good idea.
One a scale for 1 to 5, you are: 1 - 2 - 3- 4 - 5

Question 4
Taking a bath or a shower together can be very sensual.
One a scale for 1 to 5, you are: 1 - 2 - 3- 4 - 5

Score.
15 - 20: You are very much on the same level and able to read each other's signals. This will create harmony and sensuality.
10 - 14: You may be able to inspire each other and broaden the erotic horizon.
05 - 09: Hinting may not be enough. Make sure to be direct in order to avoid misunderstandings.
01 - 04: This could be a challenge, or it could be a step in to a new erotic world. It depends very much on flexibility and erotic interest.

CHAPTER 4

GENERAL STUFF

The big picture

Keep in mind that the characteristics of a Virgo may vary quite a bit depending on where within the sign she was born, as well as a wide range of additional astrological factors. But for now, let's stick to the basics. Just remember: don't jump to conclusions as soon as you meet her. Give her room to shine. Get to know the woman behind the sign.

Her personality: Pros and cons

Pros
- Natural charm
- Loyal
- Dependable
- Thorough
- Stylish and feminine
- Intelligent
- Genuine and honest
- Determined
- Compassionate
- Good sense of humour
- Down to earth
- Supportive
- Sensible

Cons
- Critical
- Uptight
- Picky
- Good girl/sacrifices herself
- Worries
- Fixed opinions
- Modest
- Stuck in her ways
- Overly health conscious
- Hung up on details
- Rigid in her ways
- High expectations of others
- Perfectionist

Tip: How to show romantic interest

Offer to help her with practical tasks.

Although independent and capable, she enjoys a man who can fix things. It makes her feel safe and protected. Afterwards, cook her something or invite her out.

Romantic Vibes

Miss Virgo:
The warm and supportive partner

The essence

Determined. She knows what she wants. This can be a blessing – and it can be a curse. In her quest for the perfect man, she follows her mind and not her heart. This may cause her to miss out on life's romantic opportunities. If she manages to let go of her romantic checklist, new opportunities will brighten her day.

Thinks twice... She's not easily carried away by romantic feelings and she will always think twice before giving in to love.

Realistic. Living on love alone is not her thing. Love may lose its sparkle, when reality sets in. However, life without love is grey and meaningless. She's a romantic in disguise.

Loving and genuine. She is affectionate and supportive. Honesty means a lot to her and an open dialogue is very important.

Strength and masculinity. Although she's very independent and strong, she needs a partner who makes her feel safe and cared for.

Affectionate. She seldom expresses feelings with words, but she will always make sure he knows how she feels about him.

Tip: How to show erotic interest

Don't be obvious about it. A gentle – and seemingly casual – massage can be a good place to start. Make sure to choose the right time, and take it slow.

Erotic Vibrations

Miss Virgo:
The cool and controlled lover

The essence

No-nonsense attitude. She sometimes asks herself: What's the big deal? She has a practical attitude to sex.

Closeness and tenderness. She prefers gentleness and closeness, and the comfort of traditional lovemaking.

Ease into it. It's important to take it slow and tune her into sex. A man who throws himself at her will simply crush her. Arousing her takes gentle patience and a touch of finesse.

No flings. She very seldom has sex with someone she meets at a party or on a first date. She needs to know him – at least a bit – and feel comfortable around him.

An amazing lover. When she finally decides to unbutton, she won't disappoint. She is feminine, gentle and loving.

No worries, no pressure. She's very understanding. Should her partner fail to get his toolbox sorted out, she will patiently arouse him until he is ready to go.

Comfort. The setting is very important. It doesn't have to be over the top, just pleasant and comfortable.

Keep it genuine. Sex should be natural and filled with joy. She will never turn sex into physical exercise.

CHAPTER 5

COMPATIBILITY QUIZ

Are you banging your head against the wall, or does she unleash your positive potential? Do you provoke her or bring out the best in her? Is she making you throw your arms into the air in exasperation, or do you feel inspired and complete in her company? Take the test to find out.

Question 1
Do you expect to go to bed with a woman on a first date?

A - Of course. When I go on a blind date, I want some fun.
B – Depends on the woman.
C - No! That's not my style. I prefer to get to know a woman before going to bed with her.

Question 2
Is a passionate partner important to you?

A - No. I believe closeness, mutual respect and intimate sex are much more important.
B - Passion is important, but not it's the most important thing.
C - Sex without passion is not sex, it's housewife aerobics.

(cont.)

Question 3.
How do you respond when your girlfriend suggests having a bath before making love?

A - That's OK I guess, I've never really thought about it. It could be fun.
B - How boring. When I'm ready for sex, I want sex not a bath!
C – Love the sensation of wet bodies against each other.

Question 4.
What do you regard as most important when entering an erotic relationship?

A - Sensuality and sensuality only.
B - Passion.
C - Compatibility - and erotic chemistry, of course.

Question 5.
You have decided to seduce you partner one evening. What do you do?

A - Stream a porn movie.
B – Make sure the setting is right… candles, soft music… the lot.
C - Buy her a bunch of flowers - and some sexy underwear.

Question 6.
Do you always expect your partner to show her feelings?

A - No. Sometimes it's better to handle your own issues without the interference from others.
B - That depends very much on the situation.
C - Of course I do. How else am I supposed to know what's on her mind?

Question 7.
Do you enjoy lots of foreplay?

A - Well, I guess that can be okay. I haven't really thought about that.
B - Yes. Foreplay makes the orgasm much more intense.
C – No. Too much foreplay makes me sleepy.

Question 8.
How do you feel about a cool and reserved woman?

A – It depends very much on the input I get – but I like a bit of mystery.
B – I avoid women like that. They annoy me.
C - Hmmm... There are many sides to a woman. A cool woman may be hiding some sparkling and hot sides to her personality....

Question 9.
Do you expect your girlfriend to take the initiative to sex?

A - Not really. Whenever we have sex it just happens.
B - Why am I supposed to take the initiative all the time?
C - I don't expect her to do so - but it's always nice when she does...

Question 10.
Have you ever caressed you partner without using your hands?

A - Without using my hands? Am I missing something here?
B - Yes, several times. It's really nice, especially when we are covered in oil...
C – Yes, when we share closeness through hugging.

SCORE	A	B	C
Question 1	1	5	10
Question 2	10	5	1
Question 3	5	1	10
Question 4	5	1	10
Question 5	1	10	5
Question 6	10	5	1
Question 7	1	10	5
Question 8	5	1	10
Question 9	10	1	5
Question 10	1	10	5

75 – 100
You have managed to find a great balance between work, sensuality and every day creativity. Even though your erotic life may not be described as hot and steamy, it's very intense and fulfilling. Sex is no big deal, as such. It's an important spice in your life, but not a hobby. This is what makes this relationship so special. Everything seems to be balanced. No matter how busy it gets, you always manage to find time for each other – to enjoy and inspire. You are on the same level and communicate with ease and love. Enjoy!

51 – 74
What have you done to her? Have you noticed the sparkle in her eyes? The enthusiasm and the happiness that surrounds her? It's called bringing out the best in people, and that's what you've managed to do. It feels so good to be on the same level with someone. To feel safe, to feel loved - to feel desired. Everything is running so smoothly. Just remember not rush her. You don't want to risk losing this unique opportunity. Sensual feelings are easily brought to life in the bathroom. Why not ask her to rub your back while taking a shower or a bath and let things develop from there... She is far more passionate than people think – and you know that.

26 – 50

If you don't share the same values. If you don't see eye to eye on the most basic questions, there will be discussions – quite a few discussions. You won't be able to move forward unless you find something that unites you, something fundamental that binds you together. Right now, you're more eager to prove you're right and try to convince the other, rather than working together. Open your mind and try to see things from different angles. Forget about right or wrong – expand your vision and your horizons. Love is a strong force. If you really feel strongly about it, bring it out and see what happens. You either move forward together or continue separately.

10 – 25

Things could probably be a lot better. Why are you sticking with her? Because she keeps your life nice and organized? How about your sex life? Not so good? Well, if sex ranks on top of your list of priorities, you're probably better off somewhere else. The two of you are so different. How you managed to get together in the first place is a great mystery. Your values are different. Your goals are different. Your needs are different… Love conquers all, but is it really love you're feeling? Maybe it's time to move on. Happiness awaits elsewhere – for both of you.

Thoughts...
It's not the score in this quiz which determines whether you will score with her. Maybe you are the jigsaw piece she is missing to make her picture complete.

Happiness is precious. If you have found happiness with her, cherish it!

LIBRA the female

YOUR DATE: LIBRA
23 September–22 October

The Essence of her

Charming – good leader and organiser – tries to please everyone and can spread herself too thin – fair and impartial – positive and constructive – intelligent – diplomatic and cooperative – values harmony, beauty and balance – forthcoming – social – charming – eloquent – feminine, sensual and erotically creative, with a passionate streak – idealistic – big-hearted – compassionate

...and remember: Never underestimate a Libra. Although she may come across as innocently flirty, this is a sharp and intelligent woman. Pay attention to her.

Blind Date – speedy essentials

Who's waiting for you?
You should be waiting for her, not the other way around. She will probably capture your attention as soon as she walks through the door. She will look beautiful and perfectly put-together: hair, makeup, outfit – and smile. Even though her clothes may be a little revealing, there's something graceful about her. She is the kind of woman who can wear a seductive outfit and still look dignified. She is aware of her beauty and the effect she has on men, and this often creates an extra sparkle in her eyes. Her manner is warm, friendly and sensual, and that usually sets the tone for the evening…

Emergency fixes for embarrassing pauses.
It's very unlikely there will be any gaps in conversation. If she likes you, she will get the dialogue going. If she feels the whole thing was a mistake, she'll be off. Even if that's the case, she may rattle on with you for a while before making an excuse. She loves interacting with people. It gives her energy and inspires her.

Your place or mine?
Either – or whichever is closest. The Libra woman is open to erotic adventures, provided that a few things are right: the mood, the setting … and the man. She is no pushover. It may take quite a while to seduce her on the first date. She must somehow feel confident that the guy will live up to her expectations. She loves the way a fling can add spice and excitement to her life, but deep down, she is secretly hoping that this man is the man

Checklist, before you dash out to meet her:
Wear a unique accessory
(hint: Show your eye for detail)
Check that your appearance is mirror-approved
(hint: Be well-groomed and attractive)
Have ideas for a surprise date suggestion
(hint: Make it intimate)
Make sure your flat is tidy, with refreshments in the fridge
(hint: In case she joins you there)
Avoid having early work the next morning
(hint: In case she stays)

Tip: Too much of a good thing is … well, too much. Balance and harmony are the essence of her life, and that applies to everything from work to love to sex.

CHAPTER 1

PREPARE YOURSELF

Catch her eye, capture her attention
Top 10 attention grabbers

1. Avoid macho moves; she prefers relaxed masculinity.
2. Admire and flatter her -- but avoid clichés. Be genuine and intelligent.
3. Tell her something unusual about yourself: an interest or a unique approach to life.
4. Show consideration for others.
5. Use a sensual voice and maintain a warm smile.
6. Items of luxury: a nice car, a watch etc.
7. Give her discreet and seductive glances.
8. Tell her about an artistic streak, whether that's a good voice, playing an instrument or being a photographer.
9. Know a thing or two about food and drink, but don't show off.
10. Be assertive – in general.

The HE. The man!

The Libra woman is looking for a man who can bring love, sensuality and balance to her life. Men often don't live up to her expectations, which is why she finds herself drifting from one to another. But it's not just the quest for her ideal mate that drives her. She is fond of men in general and loves being around them. Her friendly and playful attitude makes her very popular, and it takes a special man to pull her away from all the attention.

The Essence of him

Handsome – fit – interesting and intelligent – successful, or aspiring to be – drawn to the finer things in life – appreciates aesthetics, with an eye for beauty – generous– strong and protective – respects her need for freedom – inspiring – supportive – sensual, passionate and creative in bed – open-minded – social and friendly

---

Libra arousal meter
From 0 to 100... In 30 minutes. The setting needs to be right, and that includes her mood. It's important to take it slow and build the passion gradually.

Remember: Be true to yourself
It doesn't matter if she is the most stunning girl you've ever met – if you don't match, you don't match. You may be able to put on a show for a while to hold her attention, but what's the point? We can't please everybody. We all have different needs, dreams, tastes and preferences. There's no such thing as a one-size-fits-all lover. Be yourself, and be true to who you are – always!

Very important: Never push the Libra woman into anything. Give her time to make up her mind, or try persuading her gently by whispering in her ear. Be playful about it.

CHAPTER 2

THE FIRST DATE

**Getting your foot in the door
The basics**

No surprise visits. Thinking about popping by without advance warning? Forget it. She would hate for you to see her if she were looking scruffy.

High standards. Her outfit, makeup, hairstyle – and partner... everything needs to go well together. A date who looks like a mess won't stand a chance. A slightly dirty shirt? Don't think she won't notice - she will! In fact, the female Libra will notice details that other women would miss.

Style! She wants her partner to be as glamorous as she is – and preferably even more. If you can't afford to splash out on designer suits, at least look as though you have tried to make an effort: a nice, clean shirt, clean shave or a well-kept beard and freshly polished shoes will usually do the trick.

Artistic, sensitive - and strong! If you are a poet in disguise, let her know. She will sit down next to you and listen quietly while you recite your poems. However, sensitivity alone won't do it. She is fond of strength and masculinity. A strong body and muscular arms to hold her tight, will make her knees go wobbly.

Whatever you do...

- **DON'T** be cheap when you take her out.

- **DON'T** try to offer constructive criticism, if you've just met.

- **DON'T** make silly or crude jokes – and never on her behalf.

- **DON'T** keep her waiting for you to call, text or set up a date.

- **DON'T** give her fashion advice – unless you're a stylist.

Remember,
Even if you have managed to spark her interest, holding onto her is no easy task.

- **DON'T** be too relaxed about your looks. You won't get a second chance.

- **DON'T** talk about previous girlfriends.

- **DON'T** forget about her if you bump into people you know.

- **DON'T** underestimate her. She is smarter than you think.

- **DON'T** neglect your manners or use foul language.

Show her your masculinity and sensitive sides – and be attentive to her.

Signs you're in - or not

If you're smart and good-looking, winning her over doesn't have to be a challenge. She will often take the initiative when a man has sparked her interest. The more fascinating she finds him, the more intense her approach. She doesn't mind using her body to signal her interest. She may even dress quite seductively – but her clothes will never be cheap and tacky. If she suspects she's found the man she's been looking for, she will use every trick in the book. Still not sure if she's really interested in you? Keep an eye out for the following clues:

Chances are she will...

- be very assertive, but in a non-aggressive way
- use her sensuality to tease you
- send you short and seductive text messages
- take an interest in what you are doing
- try her best to make you proud when you're out together; act gracefully, look stunning, etc
- surprise you with an unusual gift

Not your type? Making an exit

Although the Libra woman tends to move from one partner to another, don't mistake her for a romantic drifter. She is simply looking for her dream partner, but it's no easy task. He must strike a balance of being strong and masculine while also sensitive to beauty. He must be good-looking, but not spend every evening at the gym. She may have previously thought she'd met her mate, only to discover later that he couldn't live up to her expectations. It's quite simple, really: if you're not on her level, the balance will tip, and she'll be off.

There are always exceptions. You may have met a Libra who's intensely attracted to you, who feels a harmony with you and is convinced you're the man – but if you're convinced that you're not – it may be time to dish up a dose of reality.

Foolproof exit measures:

These options will be as much a challenge for you as they will be a shock for her. Be prepared to make yourself look bad...

- Be dull and boring
- Stop paying attention to your looks ... and hygiene
- Get nosy and inquisitive about her private life
- Criticize her clothes and tell her to dress more conservatively
- Insist on keeping sex quick and sweaty, and preferably in the morning
- Ditch your manners when you're at a restaurant
- Constantly compare her to others and say you wish she was different

CHAPTER 3

SEX'N STUFF

Seductive moves:
How to get her in the mood:

Although the Libra woman is sensual and easily turned on, she is just as easily turned off. In other words, never take anything for granted. Sassy suggestions are welcome, but make sure to avoid anything crude. Feel free to surprise her, but be sensual about it. Remember, sex with her is not confined to the bedroom. Use your imagination.

Preferences and erotic nature

Flattery and admiration are the key to everything with this woman, including sex. She responds quickly to positive attention, provided the man is classy and smart. A catcall from a scruffy stranger will elicit nothing but an icy stare. Still, she sometimes gets these, because this feminine woman can be a bit of an exhibitionist – although in a subtle way. She enjoys wearing clothes that show off the curves underneath – and sometimes a little more than she intended – but she manages to do so in a classy way. She enjoys casually seducing her partner by pottering around the house in revealing clothing. She may pretend she doesn't have sex on her mind, but she knows what she's doing. Miss Libra is a sensual firework.

Hitting the right buttons

Although every sign has areas on the body that are more sensitive than others, individual sensitivity may vary quite a bit. Don't go body-blind. Honing in on these erogenous zones and forgetting the rest of her is not a good idea. Use these areas to create sparks while turning her on, and as a passion-booster when things get heated. Watch her body language – including the most obvious of signs. Open your mind to the sensuality of touch and taste.

Key areas
Her hips and buttocks

Get it on
She would probably make a good samba dancer. Moving her derrière softly and sensually comes natural to her. Many female Libras enjoy dressing to emphasize their tush. If you add the hips, you have a substantial area that's very sensitive to touch, especially a light and playful touch...

Arouse her
You can stimulate her erogenous zones in many ways, even when the two of you are out in public. For instance, you might gently caress her buttocks while your arm is draped around her waist – or carefully rub your body against her while standing in a queue. The possibilities are endless. In bed, gentle bites and a light touch of your tongue in these areas will ignite her into a firework of passion.

Surprise her
Be a little old-fashioned to keep her on her toes. Buy her a bunch of flowers or a little gift you know she'll appreciate. Although this may come across as a simply romantic gesture, her appreciation may turn sensual as soon as she gets the chance.

Spice it up
A nice massage with warm oil over her hips and buttocks will make her tingle. Use enough oil to allow your hands – or your body – glide freely over her.

Remember: She has a liberal streak and may be more adventurous than she makes herself out to be. Her flare for exhibitionism can make things interesting...

Her expectations

Take it slow. Whatever you do, never rush her. She needs to set her own pace in order to thoroughly enjoy physical encounters. Any attempt to push her into the mood for sex will only turn her off.

Ease into it. Spending a long time on foreplay is very important to her, and it should always consist of both physical and mental stimulation.

Seductive and vocal. This woman loves having sweet nothings whispered into her ear while her partner is caressing her body.

Fresh and frisky. She belongs to one of the star signs that gets a kick out of having sex in the shower. Not only does it feel good, but it gives her and her partner a chance to freshen up before taking the event to the bedroom.

No aerobics, thank you! In the Libra woman's opinion, sex should be an aesthetic experience, not a sweaty waste of time.

Show your - creative - stuff. She appreciates an inventive partner, especially if he manages to combine sensual adventures with passionate admiration.

Your sensual preferences
Quiz yourself and find out whether this woman is for you.

Where on the scale are you?
1 = Don't agree | 3 = Sure | 5 = Agree!

1. Foreplay is important. It creates intimacy and helps build passion naturally.
One a scale for 1 to 5, you are: 1 - 2 - 3- 4 - 5

2. Sex doesn't have to be confined to the bedroom, or even to the indoors...
One a scale for 1 to 5, you are: 1 - 2 - 3- 4 - 5

3. I enjoy a sensual and liberated woman who can add new dimensions to sex.
One a scale for 1 to 5, you are: 1 - 2 - 3- 4 - 5

4. Verbal communication during sex can be arousing.
One a scale for 1 to 5, you are: 1 - 2 - 3- 4 - 5

Score.
15 - 20: Sensuality, intuition and intense pleasure combine to make this relationship hot.
14–10: You will probably enter through new erotic portals with this woman and experience sex in a more sensual way.
9–5: Remember, she will notice if you start taking it easy – either when it comes to looks or sensual attention. Want to make it work? Make an effort.
4–1: Hot and steamy, or romantic and sensual? You may find yourself debating your preferences. This connection could be fun and interesting, or it could be slow and boring.

CHAPTER 4

GENERAL STUFF

The big picture

Keep in mind that the characteristics of a Libra may vary quite a bit depending on where within the sign she was born, as well as a wide range of additional astrological factors. But for now, let's stick to the basics. Just remember: don't jump to conclusions as soon as you meet her. Give her room to shine. Get to know the woman behind the sign.

Her personality: Pros and cons

Pros
- Confident about her body
- Aesthetically inclined
- Feminine and friendly
- Artistic
- Harmonious
- Sexually creative
- Erotically intuitive
- Balanced
- Attractive
- Sensual
- Positive and optimistic
- Determined
- Conscientious
- Idealistic

Cons
- Exhibitionist
- A flirt
- A serial dater
- Narcissistic
- Stubborn
- Indecisive
- Superficial
- A drifter
- Afraid of criticism
- Confrontation-avoidant
- Restless
- Moody
- Spreads herself too thin
- Fickle

Tip: How to show romantic interest

You'll need to court, romance and woo the Libra woman in the old-fashioned way. Flowers, little gifts and lots of attention will go a long way. However, be careful not to come on too strong. Play it safe, and don't rush things.

Romantic Vibes

Miss Libra:
The romantic and loving partner

The essence

That special someone... Although she's playful around men, she's idealistic about love and is always looking for that special partner who can fulfill her dreams. When she commits, her relationship needs be a source of inspiration.

No aggression, please. Arguments upset her. She would rather let things slide than get into a fight. She has the ability to see an issue from several sides, and this prevents her from jumping to conclusions.

Supportive. In order to avoid friction she needs to find a man who's on her level. As soon as she has committed to a relationship, she will be very supportive.

Keep it lively, keep it social. No matter whether she's in a relationship or not, she needs people around her.

Brighten up her spirits. She can get a little moody and restless, and a strong partner will be able to give her the strength and support she needs.

A true aesthetic. She wants a man who satisfies her need for beauty, both in his body and in his mind.

Tip: How to show erotic interest

Compliment her looks, and do it seductively. Comment on her curves, her hair and the way she carries herself. Make sure your voice is warm. Caress her with your words.

Erotic Vibrations

Miss Libra:
The aesthetic and liberated lover

The essence

Not just any setting... For romance to spark, the setting must be right. Scented candles and soppy music won't cut it. You'll need to take great care with your choice of music, wine and the atmosphere in general. A little extra attention will make a big difference.

Giving it all. She strives hard to achieve perfection, and this applies to her erotic life, as well.

Creative. She is creative and has a unique ability to turn the most traditional positions into something new and fun. Although she has some fixed ideas about sex, the Libra woman is a tolerant partner and is open to all sorts of suggestions.

Playful. She is often playful in her lovemaking. Don't be fooled into thinking that means she's inexperienced – it doesn't.

Frisky. She is a bit of an exhibitionist. She might want to arouse you by slowing stripping in front of you.

...and sensually confident. She has great confidence in her own sexuality, and she feels relaxed about it.

Make it beautiful. Be assertive in bed, but remember to be gentle, sensual and attentive. Make sex a beautiful experience.

CHAPTER 5

COMPATIBILITY QUIZ

Are you banging your head against the wall, or does she unleash your positive potential? Do you provoke her or bring out the best in her? Is she making you throw your arms into the air in exasperation, or do you feel inspired and complete in her company? Take the test to find out.

Question 1.
Do you feel appreciation for the beautiful aspects of life?

A. Absolutely. There is so much beauty in art, music and nature.
B. What beautiful aspects?
C. Sometimes, if I'm in the mood and not distracted.

Question 2.
Do you expect your partner to be explicit and assertive in bed?

A. Yes. Why should I always be the one to take charge?
B. Not at all. My partner gives me small hints, and that's good enough for me.
C. I expect her to participate actively, but nothing more.

(cont.)

Question no 3
Do you like a partner who is independent and takes care of herself?

A. Sure, but she doesn't have to be a high-flying career woman.
B. I just want her to be happy and follow her dreams. We'll support each other.
C. Yes! Then she can take care of me, too.

Question 4.
Do you ever tell your partner white lies in order to avoid conflict?

A. Yes. I hate arguments.
B. Seldom, and only very innocent ones.
C. Never. My partner is understanding, and I can discuss everything with her.

Question 5.
Do you think it's important to pursue separate interests while in a relationship?

A. Not just for the sake of it, but sure, if we have different interests.
B. No. What's the point of being in a relationship if we don't spend our time together?
C. Yes. By having separate experiences, we can grow as a couple.

Question 6.
Which of the following options would be your top choice for having sex?

A. On the beach in the moonlight.
B. In luxurious surroundings, with soft pillows and champagne.
C. In the backseat of my car.

Question no 7
Do you think it's important to romance your woman?

A. Absolutely! I'm old-fashioned when it comes to these things.
B. Not really, unless it's her birthday or a special occasion.
C. Sometimes, but it's easy to forget.

Question 8.
What does masculinity mean to you?

A. Being dominant and protective and taking care of my woman.
B. A strong mind in a strong body.
C. Being confident, and strong enough to show my sensitive side.

Question 9.
Would whispering erotic suggestions to your partner during sex be arousing for you?

A. A little. I usually do that when I'm already aroused.
B. Yes. It can add a new dimension to the experience.
C. Not really. It distracts me.

Question 10.
Are you particular about your appearance?

A. Not really, and I tend to forget to have my hair cut.
B. About average, I guess. I try to stay in shape and present myself well.
C. Absolutely. I enjoy looking good, and I have a keen eye for detail. I'm always well-groomed.

SCORE	A	B	C
Question 1	10	1	5
Question 2	1	10	5
Question 3	5	10	1
Question 4	1	5	10
Question 5	5	1	10
Question 6	10	5	1
Question 7	10	1	5
Question 8	1	5	10
Question 9	5	1	10
Question 10	1	5	10

75 – 100

Harmony, quality, excitement and intense erotic pleasure are only a few of the keywords that define this relationship – and things can stay this way, provided the two of you hold onto the feelings you are experiencing now. You share the same values and enthusiastic approach to life. You help her find her feet when her indecisiveness takes over, and she brightens your days with beauty and sensual surprises. You may be different in many areas of life, but you fulfill each other and create a rare and loving relationship.

51 – 74

The two of you have the ability to bring out the best in each other. This relationship is far too rewarding to be clouded with silly details. If problems arise, try communicating openly and gently. Never approach her with a problem and demand an opinion. Diplomacy is the key, and she'll be more than happy to discuss things with you if you choose a soft approach. Pay attention to her needs, both inside and outside the bedroom. If you're not sure how she feels about something, ask her. Never make her feel like you're taking her for granted. A nice compliment may not mean much to you, but it can make her feel incredibly good inside. Inspire her. Let both your masculine and sensitive sides shine. A strong, positive and sensual partner can make her feel relaxed and in-tune with the world.

26 – 50

You're probably feeling a little confused by this woman. What's on her mind? Where does she want to go in life? Chances are that she doesn't know herself. Sex may be fun, but it will take more than a few moments of passion to build a lasting relationship. The Libra woman can be very indecisive. She hates conflict and sometimes gets moody. Add these things together, and you have an enigma. You need to be direct with her, but try to avoid being blunt. If you're too strong, she'd rather agree than fight, and this will solve nothing. Take a constructive approach. Be attentive, positive and complimentary. Pamper her. If she still seems evasive, then it's probably time to look for happiness elsewhere.

10 – 25

Pulling your hair won't do it. You either need to become more constructive or admit that this adventure is coming to an end. You may be attracted to her for many reasons, but they may not be the right ones. Ultimately, she is probably far too evasive for you. One day she's super positive, and the next day she's not so sure. Her obsession with looks, both her own and yours, are probably driving you nuts. Is it really necessary to spend half an hour in the bathroom before nipping out to buy some milk? If you're running out of patience and not prepared to talk it all through, then this might be the end.

Thoughts...
Confused about the results in the quiz? Don't be. Only you know how you feel about this woman, and how much you are willing to work in order to make the relationship last. Be honest about your feelings and let them guide you.

SCORPIO the female

YOUR DATE: SCORPIO
23 October–21 November

The Essence of her

Guarded of her feelings – sensual – warm, with a big heart – jealous – temperamental and moody – energetic – independent – passionate about everything she does – confident and determined – choosy – interested in people, but keeps a distance until she get to know them – has a strong personality – a perfectionist, both professionally and personally

...and remember: She may be blunt at times, but don't be put off by her sharp remarks or insensitive comments. They're not intended to hurt or upset you – unless she's angry!

Blind Date – speedy essentials

Who's waiting for you?
The Scorpio woman won't be waiting for you. She won't be early, but she'll make an entrance when she does arrive. She will expect you to admire her as she enters the room – so being late, even by two minutes, is not an option! If you are, you'll be in for an awkward start to the evening, and you may find yourself kicked out before long. This woman is worth being on time for: she has a deep sensuality about her, a feminine seductiveness that men find irresistible. She's probably very attractive – not necessarily because of what she's wearing, but because of who she is.

Emergency fixes for embarrassing pauses.
You'd better hope this isn't an issue, because too many pauses will be her cue to take off, and she'll do this with icy politeness. You are supposed to entertain her, dazzle her and make her feel admired. Pauses will make her feel uneasy – and there are no second chances. Make sure the conversation is flowing casually with stories about interesting things you've seen or experienced. Allow her to interact, and never try to control the conversation. Show genuine interest. Ask intelligent questions. Need to catch your breath and gather your thoughts for a minute? Order her a glass of champagne.

Your place or mine?
Either. A luxurious hotel room might work, too. The Scorpio woman is very choosy when it comes to men, but provided a guy lives up to her standards, she doesn't mind a little passionate fun. She has a healthy appetite for sex and is attracted to men with strong, masculine bodies. No crude comments. It takes a classy man to seduce this woman.

Checklist, before you dash out to meet her:
Wear clothing that emphasises your best features
(hint: don't overdo it – be classy)
Send a text to let her know she's on your mind
(hint: keep it short and alluring)
Have a snack before you meet up
(hint: don't suggest eating right away)
Have a little extra cash on you
(hint: in case you want to treat her to something special)
Keep your cell phone on on silent
(hint: no distractions)

Tip: She can be very stubborn. Never try to *tell* her anything. Constructive criticism must be disguised as praise and suggestions.

CHAPTER 1

PREPARE YOURSELF

Catch her eye, capture her attention
Top 10 attention grabbers

1. Maintain a relaxed and friendly attitude to the people around you.
2. Have a good sense of humour, with a warm and inviting laugh.
3. Be reserved with your attention. Don't throw yourself at her.
4. Buy her a little spontaneous gift.
5. Invite her for a drink – but make it champagne, not some cheap plonk.
6. Got a body worth showing off? Show it off! (But keep it classy and subtle).
7. Let her know that you're aiming high in life – but not building castles in the air.
8. Pay her intelligent compliments in public.
9. Ask for her opinion.
10. Have a nice car, an expensive watch ... or something that indicates success.

The HE. The man!

He must be classy, strong and stylish. She needs a man she can look up to, respect and admire. Although she'd never admit it, she appreciates a steady guy who can keep her on track when her mood swings off course. Although she loves a strong body, it's love and loyalty that make the top of her list. Money and luxury is a plus, but if that's all he's got to show for himself, she'll be off.

The Essence of him
Masculine – funny, with a good sense of humour and a playful twinkle in his eyes – loyal – passionate, erotic and sensual – in control of his life, with a good job – generous; maybe even a bit extravagant at times – inspirational – understanding – intelligent – takes care of his body – attentive and admiring – reliable, no matter what

Scorpio arousal meter
From 0 to 100... At the speed of light, as long as you have connected with her and share a strong sexual chemistry

Remember: Be true to yourself

It doesn't matter if she is the most stunning girl you've ever met – if you don't match, you don't match. You may be able to put on a show for a while to hold her attention, but what's the point? We can't please everybody. We all have different needs, dreams, tastes and preferences. There's no such thing as a one-size-fits-all lover. Be yourself, and be true to who you are – always!

Very important: Don't let her run the show. If she seems bossy, it might be a test to see whether you're up to dating her. Take the initiative, be assertive and be prepared to display your masculine qualities.

CHAPTER 2

THE FIRST DATE

Getting your foot in the door
The basics

Be focused. Never glance at other women when courting her. She is jealous and won't tolerate a date who's a little too friendly with other women.

Take her seriously. Don't make fun of her opinions. You can question them – but only if you're intelligent about it and have something to offer.

...and be sincere! You won't charm her by throwing compliments around. She can tell the difference between a sincere compliment and a clever tactic to get into her bed.

Treat her. When inviting her out, don't be a cheapskate! Food trucks and fast food joints will be regarded as insults – unless you have something interested lined up afterwards.

Make it special. When courting a female Scorpio, you need to show her that you have made an effort to please her in some way – a romantic home cooked meal, for example.

Be attentive. Listen, ask questions and don't criticise. Pay attention to her: what she does, what she says – everything.

Whatever you do...

- **DON'T** flirt with – or even glance at – other women.

- **DON'T** take her interest for granted.

- **DON'T** be cheap. Pamper her.

- **DON'T** talk about previous girlfriends.

- **DON'T** criticise her views or tell her to do things differently.

Remember, especially if you've just met, never take anything for granted. She won't keep a

- **DON'T** leave all the decisions to her.

- **DON'T** change your plans at the last minute – unless you have a very good reason.

- **DON'T** tell white lies on order to impress her.

- **DON'T** comment on other women's appearance.

- **DON'T** make promises you can't keep, no matter how small.

man around if he fails to show loads of attention and admiration.

Signs you're in - or not

A Scorpio woman knows exactly how to seduce a man. It's not just her outfit – although it will probably be feminine, seductive and even a little provocative – but rather her eyes, voice and the way she carries herself that makes men pay the most attention. She will smile, flirt, tease and charm you and capture your interest – only to turn around and casually start flirting with someone else. If you're hooked, you'll find yourself striving to hold onto her attention – and that's exactly what she wants: men fighting for her. However, if she really likes you, she won't risk losing you. Her playful interest in other men is merely an effort to sharpen your appetite for her. Unsure about whether her interest is genuine? Look out for the following:

Chances are she will...

- be available when you call
- cancel dates with friends to be with you
- act seductive and take the initiative to be intimate
- be protective towards you ... and fend off other women
- ask what you're up to, casually making sure there's no competition
- make an effort to please you: preparing food, giving you a massage, etc.

Not your type? Making an exit

When a Scorpio woman gives into love, she gives in completely. There is no such thing as 50% commitment in her world – and that applies to romance. She will bond with her man on a very deep level, and when that happens, this flirtatious woman transforms into an incredibly loyal and supportive partner. She will admire him in public, compliment his masculinity and make herself attractive to him in every way. If things are going well, the female Scorpio will make her man the focal point of her life.

If she has really bonded with her partner, she will try her best to make things work – even if that means adjusting her ways. But there are limits to everything, even for a Scorpio in love. If she's not ready to leave, things will get stormy. Eventually, she'll probably give you a verbal black eye, break a few plates, gather her things and slam the door behind her.

Foolproof exit measures:

Remember, she feels passionately about everything. Don't go ahead with these steps unless you are prepared for some emotional blowback.

- Tell her to dress more appropriately and stop looking so cheap
- Never discuss anything with her. You're going to do things your way, and that's it
- Prioritise TV and burgers instead of going to the gym
- Tell her to slow down in bed
- Flirt with other women at the grocery store, the restaurant, the bar, the library…
- Question all of her suggestions and argue whenever possible.

CHAPTER 3

SEX'N STUFF

Seductive moves:
How to get her in the mood:

Sexual chemistry is very important. A Scorpio woman can immediately sense when a man is interested in her, and this spark will soon develop into a burning sexual desire. Miss Scorpio responds well to a man who can say everything she wants to hear by staring into her eyes and whispering erotic suggestions into her ear.

Preferences and erotic nature

Sex is very important to her, and she expects quite a bit from her lover. For one thing, he must display his passionate and sensual sides with ease and confidence. She enjoys getting sexual hints, no matter how small. Don't wait until the two of you are in the bedroom. An erotic encounter with a female Scorpio usually starts several hours before you end up together in bed. Keep this in mind when you're out having dinner. Enjoy your food slowly and seductively and touch her leg with your foot – in other words, communicate with your body language that you're dying to rip her clothes off.

Hitting the right buttons

Although every sign has areas on the body that are more sensitive than others, individual sensitivity may vary quite a bit. Don't go body-blind. Honing in on these erogenous zones and forgetting the rest of her is not a good idea. Use these areas to create sparks while turning her on, and as a passion-booster when things get heated. Watch her body language – including the most obvious of signs. Open your mind to the sensuality of touch and taste.

Key areas
Her private parts

Get it on
Although she has an erotic nature, she doesn't like guys who are blunt and obvious about their advances. But don't worry – there are ways to stimulate her without offending her.

Arouse her
Gently press your body and pelvic area against her when standing in a queue. Arrange her napkin on her lap while having dinner and let your hand linger. If the mood is right and you've sparked her erotic interest, it won't take much friction to turn her on.

Surprise her
You can surprise her by slight modifications to your attitude. Allow your glance to linger a little longer, brush your fingers over her arm and smile seductively. Hold onto the intensity. She will play along as soon as she has picked up on the erotic vibes – and it won't take long.

Spice it up
Add a hint of something forbidden, like a public place (a slight erotic touch when no one is looking, perhaps). Another option might be to arouse her during working hours with a seductive phone call.

Remember: She's not into quickies – to her, they're like grabbing some fast food instead of enjoying a gourmet meal. In other words: if you're in a hurry, don't suggest having sex.

Her expectations

Whispers. Excite her mind. Not familiar with the magic of whispering sensual suggestions into your partner's ear? Start practicing. She is turned on by 'verbal erotics' and the seductive sound of her partner's voice. Sex, to her, is far more than a physical action. Erotic sensations excite her mind as well as her body.

Turn it around. She enjoys experimenting with positions, sexual gadgets – you name it, she'll try it – or at least consider trying it...

Fast mover. When she wants you, she wants you now. Be prepared for sexual action when you least expect it. And keep in mind that she doesn't handle rejection well...

Intense. She has an incredible ability to prolong intercourse by holding back her climax, which can often drive her partner into an intense state of passion.

Bring out the masculinity. Her dream partner is masculine, intense and passionate. He must be erotically adventurous, attentive to her needs and possess a lot of patience and endurance.

Your sensual preferences
Quiz yourself and find out whether this woman is for you.

Where on the scale are you?
1 = Don't agree | 3 = Sure | 5 = Agree!

1. The build-up to sex may start several hours before getting physically intimate.
One a scale for 1 to 5, you are: 1 - 2 - 3- 4 - 5

2. It's impossible to stimulate the body without stimulating the mind.
One a scale for 1 to 5, you are: 1 - 2 - 3- 4 - 5

3. Being expressive and vocal in bed can increase erotic sensations.
One a scale for 1 to 5, you are: 1 - 2 - 3- 4 - 5

4. Quick sex can never replace passionate sensuality.
One a scale for 1 to 5, you are: 1 - 2 - 3- 4 - 5

Score.
15 - 20: You likely share strong sexual chemistry and a fundamental desire for passion and erotic adventures. Enjoy!
14–10: This relationship is sure to include exciting sex – and many opportunities for you to display your passionate side.
9 – 5: You can either give up and get run over, or give in and open your mind to a new world of passionate pleasures.
4–1: This woman may take sex a little more seriously than you do. When she makes love, she gives herself over completely to her partner. Allow yourself to fully experience her.

CHAPTER 4

GENERAL STUFF

The big picture

Keep in mind that the characteristics of a Scorpio may vary quite a bit depending on where within the sign she was born, as well as a wide range of additional astrological factors. But for now, let's stick to the basics. Just remember: don't jump to conclusions as soon as you meet her. Give her room to shine. Get to know the woman behind the sign.

Her personality: Pros and cons

Pros
- Sensual
- Independent
- Passionate
- Committed
- Choosy
- Confident
- Has a strong personality
- A perfectionist
- Sensitive
- Attractive
- Cool and mysterious
- Intelligent
- Compassionate
- Intuitive

Cons
- Jealous
- Reserved
- Suspicious
- Temperamental
- Emotional
- Stubborn
- Sarcastic when provoked
- Seldom forgives and forgets
- Rigid in her views
- Weary of losing control
- Has tunnel vision
- Vengeful
- Demanding
- Calculating

Tip: How to show romantic interest

Try an old-fashioned approach. Call her, invite her out and bring her a little gift – but don't overdo it. Allow her to be intrigued and fascinated by you.

Romantic Vibes

Miss Scorpio:
The intense and committed partner

The essence

Strong feelings. The Scorpio woman feels everything intensely. Either she's in love, or she's not. When a man captures her heart, she'll be completely absorbed by him.

High expectations. She expects a lot of attention from her man. This is why her romances either yield intense relationships – or fail completely. A man who can't handle her intensity will be off pretty quickly.

Don't smooth it over. She doesn't respond well to emotional bribery. After a fight, an attempt to smooth things over with a gift or bunch of flowers will only make matters worse. Instead, he should tell her he's sorry – and why. He needs to let her know that he's aware he messed up and is prepared to do something about it.

100% committed. When a Scorpio woman commits to a man, the relationship engulfs her life. Friends may begin to hear from her less.

Royal treatment. She is very loyal and will pamper, support and show admiration for her partner, both privately and in public – just as long as he doesn't start glancing at other women...! Beware a jealous woman's fury.

Tip: How to show erotic interest

She is intuitive and picks up on hints very quickly. A surprising phone call to ask how she's doing – using a warm and sensual voice – will be enough to convey your message...

Erotic Vibrations

Miss Scorpio:
The passionate and hot lover

The essence

No quickies. Never build her anticipation for sex without delivering. And don't try to wiggle your way out of it by suggesting a quick one. If you've only just met, she'll probably ditch you and look for a more passionate guy.

***The* seductress.** When she's made up her mind about seducing a man, she rarely fails. It takes significant self-control to resist her voice and hypnotic eyes.

Don't put on a show. There's nothing casual about her sex life. To her, having sex means giving 100%. If not, you might as well be watching TV.

Bring out the passion! She is a demanding lover with loads of energy and endurance. She will take it as a personal insult if you turn your back on her after only 15 minutes of intense lovemaking.

Erotic wavelength. If you manage to establish a strong sensual chemistry with her, she will treat you like a king and pamper you in every possible way, not only sexually.

CHAPTER 5

COMPATIBILITY QUIZ

Are you banging your head against the wall, or does she unleash your positive potential? Do you provoke her or bring out the best in her? Is she making you throw your arms into the air in exasperation, or do you feel inspired and complete in her company? Take the test to find out.

Question no 1
You are having a wonderful time at a party and feeling great. What would you do if your girlfriend accused you of flirting with other women?

A – That would never happen because I would never do anything to make her feel insecure. I'm friendly with both men and women, but I never flirt.
B – Just typical! I might as well sit down in a corner and sulk.
C – I would put my arms around her and use my body language to reassure her that although many women are there, she is the woman.

Question no 2
What kind of woman do you prefer? Someone who's open, frank and straight to the point, or someone who's slightly mysterious?

A – I'm no mind reader. I like women who won't leave me guessing.
B – A little bit of both, really. It depends on the woman.
C – I love mysterious women. They are like treasure chests, waiting to be discovered and explored.

(cont.)

Question no 3
Have you ever been tempted to test a woman's love for you by flirting with others?

A – Of course. It's the only way to find out how she feels about me.
B – No, never. If I care about her, why would I want to make her feel jealous?
C – Sometimes, but only for fun – never anything serious.

Question no 4
How do you respond when your partner decides to change your erotic routine and introduce something new?

A - Great! I'd love that.
B - I wouldn't like that. I prefer the quiet comforts of sex.
C – It'd be fine, provided it gives us both pleasure.

Question no 5
Would you consider yourself mentally strong?

A – Yo, stupid question! I'm one of the strongest guys at the gym!
B – Yes, although we all have our ups and downs. Generally, I'm not easily pushed off balance.
C – I've never really thought about it. About average, I guess.

Question no 6
Would you keep in touch with your female friends after starting a new relationship?

A – No, that would feel a bit awkward.
B – Yes, but on a different level – and not often. I would always be open about it, too.
C - Yes! I like women, and I don't want to lose friends just for the sake of a relationship. I would also stay in touch with ex-girlfriends.

Question no 7
Do you often find yourself in heated debates?

A – Yes, I have strong opinions about most things.
B – No. I'm not easily provoked.
C – Not often, but sometimes – only if the topic is important to me.

Question no 8
You have planned to go out with the guys. How would you respond if your girlfriend looked at you seductively and said, 'I thought we might have some alone time tonight?'

A - She sometimes does that, but I don't care. I'd go out with the guys anyway.
B – Hmm ... this is a difficult one. It would depend on what we'd had planned.
C - I would probably cancel on the guys. She can be very seductive and persuasive.

Question no 9
Have you ever turned a woman on without seeing it through?

A – No, never. I'd hate it if she did that to me.
B - Sure, I'm a handsome guy. Plus, she's easily aroused, and I can't be expected to deliver 24/7.
C - Very seldom, and only if I've been in a hurry, or we've been out in public or something like that.

Question no 10
Do you think it's okay to have a fling with a stranger when you're dating another woman?

A - No problem. Life is for living, and I've got a great appetite for sex.
B - It depends on who committed to the woman.
C – Nope! Never!

SCORE	A	B	C
Question 1	10	1	5
Question 2	1	5	10
Question 3	1	10	5
Question 4	5	1	10
Question 5	1	10	5
Question 6	10	5	1
Question 7	5	10	1
Question 8	1	5	10
Question 9	10	1	5
Question 10	1	5	10

75 – 100

You have either cheated during the quiz to get optimal answers – or else entered one of the most rewarding, exciting, loving, passionate and sexiest relationships out there. You can communicate without uttering a single word – sometimes even a glance and a smile is enough. She is sharp, independent, loyal and passionate, and she manages to bring out the fire on you – on many levels. You respect and admire each other. Everything feels right. The base for this relationship is strong. Enjoy it.

51 – 74

Loads of fun. Loads of sex. Loads of passion and excitement. You have captured a woman who is energetic and demanding, and you know exactly how to handle her. Boredom will never be a problem for you two. You share her enthusiasm for keeping life interesting, so it's no wonder that every day seems like a new adventure. You may experience a fight from time to time, but don't be put off. The female Scorpio will apologise when she realises that she has done you wrong – even if it takes her weeks or months to admit it. Keep in mind that this woman needs to be on her own every now and then. Don't take it personally; it's got nothing to do with you. Let her have her moments of solitude, and she'll return to you as soon as she's recharged her mental battery.

26 – 50

What made you enter into a relationship with her? Her body and passionate sensuality? Either you're a very patient guy, or you have come across a rare flexible Scorpio. It's time to figure out what you're looking for in a woman and what makes you happy – as well as whether you have what makes her happy. The female Scorpio needs support from a caring partner. This means a few things for you: try to ignore her fierce temper. Don't always try to persuade her that you're right. Don't be too independent – but don't be too dependent, either. Respond with humour when you want to respond with anger. Support her, even when you're tempted to throw your hands in the air. Who knows, she may turn out to be the woman after all.

10 – 25

The magic has disappeared like the morning dew from a flower. She is probably not the woman you thought she was. It doesn't matter that she makes you feel like a king in bed if the bliss disappears as soon as the alarm clock goes off. You're disconnected on many levels, and her expectations and values are different to yours. The constant tension will begin to wear you out after a while. Do you regularly misunderstand each other? Communicate. If the disagreements are non-negotiable, then it might be best to hunt for happiness elsewhere.

Thoughts...
Don't make assumptions. Make sure you are moving in the same direction. Not sure where you are going? Ask her.

SAGITTARIUS the female

YOUR DATE: SAGITTARIUS
22 November–21 December

The Essence of her

Sparkling, cheerful and optimistic... she's a breath of fresh air – direct and outspoken – she'll jump onto the barricades to fight for people she cares about – doesn't take herself too seriously – she doesn't really care about what other people might think – independent and intelligent – defines her own path in life – determined – open and social – unsnobbish, both when it comes to people and possessions

...and remember: She'll be more than happy to give you advice, providing you don't return the next day complaining about the same problem. She will probably wonder why you didn't get the message the first time, and tell you off. She is not insensitive, she just can't stand pessimists.

Blind Date – speedy essentials

Who's waiting for you?
She will greet you with a big smile. Never mind if you're a little late, she's there to have fun and enjoy herself, and there is no room for a muggy attitude. Apart from her beautiful smile, you'll notice how attractive she is. Her hair, regardless of whether it's long or short, will be shiny and healthy. Her outfit is a perfect balance of colours and textures. You can tell she has made an effort. What really captures your attention is her sparkling and positive personality. She seems genuinely thrilled to see you, and she probably is!

Emergency fixes for embarrassing pauses.
When her gaze becomes unfocused and her eyes start wandering around the room, it's a sign that her concentration is slipping, most likely because she's not particularly interested in what you're saying. However, this doesn't mean she's not interested in you. The best way to make her regain her focus is by asking her questions about something she's done or something she's interested in

Your place or mine?
Either. Or some other place if it's more convenient! She is fascinated by men and loves sex. If she's erotically attracted to a man, she sees no reason why she shouldn't have sex with him. But, even though she may show erotic interest in him, she can become disinterested just as quickly. Sparking her interest is the easy part – holding on to it is the real challenge.

Checklist, before you dash out to meet her:
• Have a coffee – be alert!
(hint: Show off your sharp mind.)
 Have a fun suggestion for you to do
(hint: Surprise her)
• Have some good (positive!) stories
(hint: Entertain her)
• Make good puns and wordplay
(hint: Be humorous – and smart)
• Wear attire that emphasises your body – the good parts
(hint: Don't overdo it)

Tip: She can be a tease. Playing hard to get, or indicating that she's more interested than she really is, is her way to check out a guy before making her mind up about an erotic fling.

CHAPTER 1

PREPARE YOURSELF

Catch her eye, capture her attention
Top 10 attention grabbers

1. An unusual invitation, like a Japanese evening at your place, etc.
2. Flattery, but not in an obvious way. Be smart about it.
3. A positive attitude towards life in general. No complaints.
4. Tell her about interesting things you have done or seen.
5. Be charming, forthcoming and a little cool.
6. Being inclusive and striking up friendly conversations with people around you.
7. Suggest trying some new and interesting food.
8. Not taking yourself too seriously.
9. Slight erotic hints with a humorous edge.
10. Not being afraid to display relaxed masculinity.

The HE. The man!

He must be confident and able to handle a free-spirited woman without displaying any trace of jealousy or possessiveness. He must be strong and independent, attentive, inspiring and caring. Having an excellent sense of humour goes without saying, but he needs to be smart and intelligent too. She needs someone who can inspire and stimulate her. He really needs to be on his toes... or she'll be off as soon as it gets boring.

The Essence of him
Enthusiastic with a positive outlook on life – intelligent and with his head in the right place – down to earth, but adventurous – able to discover excitement in everyday activities – sensual and erotic – spontaneous – independent and respectful of her need for freedom – works out and looks after his body – if not successful, at least has a vision of what he would like to do or achieve in life.

Sagittarius arousal meter
From 0 to 100... In 10 minutes – providing you've got her attention. She loves sex and is very impulsive – also when it comes to time and place.

Remember: Be true to yourself

It doesn't matter if she is the most stunning girl you've ever met – if you don't match, you don't match. You may be able to put on a show for a while to hold her attention, but what's the point? We can't please everybody. We all have different needs, dreams, tastes and preferences. There's no such thing as a one-size-fits-all lover. Be yourself, and be true to who you are – always!

Very important: She is a free spirit. Any attempt to tie her down will make her wriggle free and take off. Her love and loyalty thrive with freedom.

CHAPTER 2

THE FIRST DATE

Getting your foot in the door
The basics

No time-wasters, please! The female Sagittarius has a great appetite for men, but she will never waste time on a bore!

Jump in. She doesn't mind taking chances, and that includes her love life as well. She won't analyze a guy for ages. If she has fallen for a particular side to his personality, she will take a chance on him.

A bit of action. She loves fun and excitement. Too many evenings at home will freak her out.

Sharp and smart. Let her know you have an alert mind.

Be attentive. Listen to all the things she tells you (which will be an awful lot...) and give her your opinion.

Humour is the key. The female Sagittarius hates pessimistic guys, so take your problems and get gloomy somewhere else.

Be enthusiastic, and she will soon get enthusiastic about you.

Whatever you do...

- **DON'T** be jealous and possessive.

- **DON'T** be envious and criticize successful people.

- **DON'T** be easily offended.

- **DON'T** suggest traditional date things, unless with a twist.

- **DON'T** be pessimistic about the future.

Remember, although you like her, keep her guessing a little. She enjoys a challenge. Be careful and don't pull it too far.

- **DON'T** tease her with old-fashioned gender roles. She doesn't find that funny!

- **DON'T** plan the evening down to the last detail.

- **DON'T** be too physical, putting your arm around her, etc.

- **DON'T** tell her lame jokes.

- **DON'T** try to impress her with white lies.

If she has to wait too long for you to make a move, she will continue on to the next interesting guy in her life.

Signs you're in - or not

Even though she shows interest in you, never take anything for granted. If she's not 100% sure about you, she will play it safe and keep a friendly distance. However, she will sometimes do the same when she is interested... Hello, confusion! If you have managed to spin her head around, she will probably take the initiative to do something. She'd rather make a move than risk some other woman stealing you away. She seldom relies on suggestive outfits and seductive glances. Her approach will always be positive and friendly. Keep a lookout for the following:

Chances are she will...

- approach you directly and ask you out
- take an interest in what you do and who you are
- be extra charming and sparkling around you
- give you direct, sensual hints
- organize a get-together and make sure you're invited
- give you her positive opinions on your work or ideas

Not your type? Making an exit

If you find yourself wanting out of a relationship with a female Sagittarius, you've probably cast a spell on her. This woman will often have left a long time before conflicts reach the surface. She needs positivity and adventure; she needs inspiration, freedom and excitement. Life without impulsiveness and spontaneity drains her. Leaving a lover or a partner is usually no big deal – unless the relationship has taken a more committed turn. She will simply move on to the next romantic adventure in her life.

If she sticks around, and sticks around, and sticks around… you might want to send her a clear message. Make sure to be consistent. If you're not, she might just think you're just having a bad day and give you another chance.

Foolproof exit measures:

You don't really need to be blunt about it: being possessive and restricting her freedom will usually do the trick.

- Tell her you're tired of her being a social butterfly
- Criticize her for being disorganized
- Be pessimistic about everything
- Insist on sex the same way, on the same day
- Make sure to plan everything, even the trip to the supermarket
- Question her positive outlook and offer a more "realistic" view

CHAPTER 3

SEX'N STUFF

Seductive moves:
How to get her in the mood:

She is easily turned on – and off. It doesn't take much to get her in the mood, but the challenge is keeping her there. Her partner needs to be enthusiastic and erotic. If he leans back and expects her to run the show, there will be a no-show from her. She'll be off watching TV or on her way to hang out with her friends.

Preferences and erotic nature

She enjoys teasing her partner, not only during foreplay but also during intercourse. When her partner is about to come, she will probably hold back a little, wait and then move on again. This may seem a little cruel, but the climax will be a firework. Many female Sagittarians are turned on by the idea of having sex outside, in a secluded public place – preferably out in nature. She is no exhibitionist, she simply loves the excitement and the sensation of cool, outside air against her body.

Hitting the right buttons

Although every sign has areas on the body that are more sensitive than others, individual sensitivity may vary quite a bit. Don't go body-blind. Honing in on these erogenous zones and forgetting the rest of her is not a good idea. Use these areas to create sparks while turning her on, and as a passion-booster when things get heated. Watch her body language – including the most obvious of signs. Open your mind to the sensuality of touch and taste.

Key areas
Her hips and thighs

Get it on
The key is not to be too obvious about it. Avoid clumsy fondling under the table while you're having dinner in a restaurant. When you're focusing on her hips and thighs, your touch needs to be gentle and sensual.

Arouse her
If you are in bed together, you will soon discover that gentle bites, passionate kisses and playful flicks with your tongue over the inside of her thighs will make her breathe heavily. But, while it feels nice and arouses her, she doesn't want you to keep at it forever – if you don't move on, she might get bored and the hot feelings will cool down. Make sure to read her signals and her body language.

Surprise her
She has another erogenous zone: her hair. When other women would have gone off to sleep while having their hair stroked and played with, this woman will wake up with an erotic twinkle in her eyes...

Spice it up
If she's not used to watching herself having sex, give it a try. Add a few large mirrors in the bedroom and quite a few candles. Although she will be fascinated by the experience, she's also very vain. Make sure she gets to admire herself in a flattering light.

Remember: She is quite liberal and will get bored if her partner fails to inspire her. Try slight adjustments to the erotic routine, or take the initiative when she least expects it.

Her expectations

Get moving. Forget foreplay that goes on forever. The female Sagittarius is usually eager to move on to the real thing!

Add spice. Sex with her is not a one-minute stunt. Far from it. She enjoys intercourse very much and is eager to try out different variations.

Be creative. She is playful in bed and expects her partner to be likewise. Creativity is a great plus. New ideas will always be appreciated and eagerly tried out – providing they are not vulgar!

Well, why not…? She has a strong liberal streak, and with the right encouragement, she may consider exploring some of your erotic fantasies.

Afterplay. Never turn your back on her and go to sleep. She appreciates a little chat afterwards, maybe with a glass of wine, to share feelings – an extended version of "it was good for me, was it good for you'?" Maybe not all that romantic, but very nice and quite informative.

Your sensual preferences
Quiz yourself and find out whether this woman is for you.

Where on the scale are you?
1 = Don't agree | 3 = Sure | 5 = Agree!

1. Too much foreplay takes the passion out of sex.
One a scale for 1 to 5, you are: 1 - 2 - 3- 4 - 5

2. Sex without creativity will get very boring in the long run.
One a scale for 1 to 5, you are: 1 - 2 - 3- 4 - 5

3. Closeness during sex tends to feel a little claustrophobic.
One a scale for 1 to 5, you are: 1 - 2 - 3- 4 - 5

4. Impulsiveness is important, as well as being open to having sex in different places.
One a scale for 1 to 5, you are: 1 - 2 - 3- 4 - 5

Score.
15 - 20: Wow. Erotic fireworks will be crackling!
10 - 14: This may be a little more adventurous than what you're used to. Open your mind and expand your erotic horizons. You'll enjoy it.
05 - 09: If you feel she's moving a little too fast, don't tell her to pace herself. Suggest trying something different, something slower, and make it sound like an adventure.
01 - 04: This may be an adventure or it could be a complete miss. You will either inspire each other or turn each other off.

CHAPTER 4

GENERAL STUFF

The big picture

Keep in mind that the characteristics of a Sagittarius may vary quite a bit depending on where within the sign she was born, as well as a wide range of additional astrological factors. But for now, let's stick to the basics. Just remember: don't jump to conclusions as soon as you meet her. Give her room to shine. Get to know the woman behind the sign.

Her personality: Pros and cons

Pros
- Very optimistic
- Compassionate
- Intelligent
- Independent
- Clear and alert-minded
- Problem solver
- Outspoken
- Creative
- Charming
- Attractive
- Original
- Choosy

Cons
- Fear of failure
- Sore loser
- Absentminded
- Restless and impatient
- Loses interest quickly
- Changes sex partners often
- Wary of romantic commitment
- Blunt and insensitive
- Sarcastic
- Hurtfully honest
- Arrogant
- Vain

Tip: How to show romantic interest

Surprise her with an invitation or arrange something she'll truly appreciate. Even though it may involve other people, the fact that you made an effort will make her see you in a very positive light.

Romantic Vibes

Miss Sagittarius:
The enthusiastic and optimistic partner

The essence

Never take anything for granted. You may be able to spark her interest, but she won't hang around if there's no point spending time on you. A cheerful goodbye, and she'll be off to her next romantic encounter. If you want to hold on to this woman, you need to live up to her expectations.

Loves men. She often moves from one man to the next, simply because she finds men fascinating. Entering a committed relationship requires a very special man.

What you see is what you get. Some men have probably been either discouraged or surprised by the fact that she won't change. Relationship or not, she remains who she is. No, she won't be unfaithful, but she'll insist on keeping in touch with her friends – male and female.

Freedom. She enjoys pursuing interests on her own and expects her partner to do the same. She loves spending time with her man, but she will never cling to him. A flexible partner will bring out the warmth and love in her.

Celebrate! The female Sagittarius loves fun and entertainment. Grab any opportunity to celebrate and throw parties. Be social, adventurous and fun! A bit hectic? Just go for it: your reward will be a devoted woman.

Tip: How to show erotic interest

Be impulsive about it. Be playful and a little cheeky. Suggest an intimate flirt in an unusual place… and get her imagination going. Avoid erotic suggestions when she's busy. Either she won't notice or she'll get annoyed.

Erotic Vibrations

Miss Sagittarius:
The playful and creative lover

The essence

Sassy ideas. She's always on the move, both physically and mentally. Her mind is filled with ideas – erotic ones too!

A little fresh air... If she could, she would probably want to make love outdoors. Although she's no exhibitionist, she can get a kick from knowing that somebody might be watching.

Keep up with her. Don't expect her to be patient and tolerant if you want to drag it out and take your time. If you fail to satisfy her, she might lose her spark.

No distracting emotions. You may get the impression that she is holding back emotionally, which might be true. She is not particularly keen on bringing romantic feelings into her erotic world. She prefers sex to be fun and adventurous, not romantic and soppy. In fact, friendly feelings are far more important to her when having sex than romantic love.

Why be boring? She is adventurous in bed and dislikes erotic routines. Due to her restless personality, she is likely to move on to a new man if her partner gets too boring.

CHAPTER 5

COMPATIBILITY QUIZ

Are you banging your head against the wall, or does she unleash your positive potential? Do you provoke her or bring out the best in her? Is she making you throw your arms into the air in exasperation, or do you feel inspired and complete in her company? Take the test to find out.

Question 1.
Do you regard yourself as impulsive or do you need to plan everything?

A. I prefer to organize my days.
B. It all depends, really. I am impulsive, but certain things must be planned in advance.
C. I'm very impulsive and I embrace life's opportunities whenever I can.

Question 2.
New ideas, impulsiveness, enthusiasm… How do these fit into your erotic world?

A. Very well. I love the excitement!
B. I enjoy variation as erotic spice, but not variation just for the sake of it.
C. Sex to me is intimacy and tenderness, not breath-taking activities.

(cont.)

Question 3.
How do you feel about a woman who always speaks her mind?

A. It's refreshing, but maybe a little annoying at times.
B. I like a woman who's straight with me and gives me her opinions. It creates openness and trust.
C. You can't just blurt something out anytime. Being diplomatic is very important.

Question 4.
The two of you are going to a dinner party and you've just been told that you have to wait half an hour for the taxi to arrive. What do you do when she suggests that you might as well get comfortable...?

A. Smile and start unbuttoning her blouse...
B. Become really stressed, and start putting your coat on.
C. Kiss her and say, "Nice try... better wait till later."

Question 5.
When a woman is sensually teasing you, do you expect her to deliver?

A. Yes, of course. Never start anything you don't intend to finish.
B. Yes, but I need to play an active part too in order to make it happen.
C. Yes and no. Flirting takes on many forms. An innocent flirt doesn't have to be an erotic invitation.

Question 6.
Does a frank and outspoken woman appeal to you?

A. Honesty is important, but honesty also hurts.
B. Yes. This leaves me in no doubt where I stand with her.
C. No! I hate to be told I've made a mistake or I look a mess.

Question 7.
Do you sometimes do crazy things in order to get a new erotic experience?

A. I must admit that I do – life is for living!
B. Never. Sex is not supposed to be some sort of sport.
C. On rare occasions, yes. But only when I'm in the mood or with the right partner.

Question 8.
Are you a slow mover or do you tend to get easily aroused?

A. I'm definitely a slow mover; I prefer long foreplay in order to get really hot.
B. That depends very much on the mood and the shape I'm in.
C. I'm definitely not a slow mover. When I'm hot, I want action – NOW!

Question 9.
Do you mind being chatted up by a woman?

A. Not at all. That's a great compliment. I love assertive women.
B. Yes, I don't like aggressive women.
C. That would depend very much on the woman, and whether I like her or not.

Question 10.
Do you feel happy about other people's success?

A. No. It usually reminds me of my failures and shortcomings.
B. Sometimes; depends on who it is and whether I like the person.
C. Of course. Being happy on behalf of others means I'm happy, right?

SCORE	A	B	C
Question 1	1	5	10
Question 2	10	5	1
Question 3	5	10	1
Question 4	10	1	5
Question 5	10	5	1
Question 6	5	10	1
Question 7	10	1	5
Question 8	1	5	10
Question 9	10	1	5
Question 10	1	5	10

75 – 100

You'll never be bored as long as you stick with your female Sagittarius. Never! It doesn't matter what you do, every day will be filled with some sort of adventure. She doesn't need to fly around the world to experience excitement, she has the unique ability to bring out adventure in everyday activities – and you love it! Impulsiveness is important for both of you, and you cherish the ideas you give each other. You may be quite different, but the difference makes you grow. You know how to handle her restless nature and make her feel safe and happy. She comes to you for sensual inspiration and guidance, and you never disappoint her. This can be a very rewarding relationship.

51 – 74

Smart, intelligent, super positive and enthusiastic, she is a treasure chest of inspiration and wonderful feelings! You have the ability to keep her grounded without making her feel trapped and stressed. She kicks your butt when you're feeling lazy and unmotivated, and you make her take a deep breath from time to time and look around her. There may be a few discussions, but that only keeps the relationship fresh and exciting. You don't have to tag along with her all the time. Grant yourself a time-out once in a while and catch your breath. She may be a little exhausting at times – but boring? Never!

26 – 50
This could be a challenge. It could be a positive one or you could find yourself banging your head against the wall. Whenever you want a quiet and sensual moment with her in bed, she suggests a quick one on the kitchen table. A romantic evening can suddenly turn into a bring-your-own-pizza-and-wine party with her friends. You never really know what's going to happen. Which is what makes her so special – and draining. In order to experience complete happiness, you need to be able to keep up with her. Sure, you might ask her to slow down a bit, and she may even do so for a little while, but it's against her nature and it won't last. Regard her as an opportunity to spice up your life and broaden your horizons. You can either take the chance or let it pass you by

10 – 25
She may have dazzled you with her enthusiasm, optimism and charm some time ago, but how do you feel now? Stressed out? Frustrated? Overlooked? Either she's off with her friends, busy with some new activity, or she hassles you for not being more active. Whenever you want to take it easy, she's got some new idea popping into her mind. It's almost impossible to plan anything: everything from sex to everyday activities happens at the spur of the moment! You never really know what to expect, or when to expect it. She is an amazing woman, but the two of you may find yourselves on different levels. If you manage to open your mind and release a little more energy into your life, you may find her exciting. If that's not your thing, she will probably drain you.

Thoughts...
No matter what you decide to do, make sure to do it for the right reasons. Let your heart guide you, and let your mind adjust the course.

CAPRICORN the female

YOUR DATE: CAPRICORN
22 December–19 January

The Essence of her

Stylish – feminine – persistent– independent, but longing for a strong and protective man by her side – ambitious – a passionate lover – perfectionistic – loyal and reliable – efficient – optimistic – snobbish – reserved before she gets to know someone – stubborn –intelligent – has an eye for beauty and quality in everything around her – hard-working

...and remember: Although she may come across as cool and reserved, she is warm, genuine and affectionate when you get to know her.

Blind Date – speedy essentials

Who's waiting for you?
She might be a little early, but she's usually right on time. If you're not there, she will start wondering if she got the time messed up. She's reluctant to think you're sloppy and not able to keep a date. In other words: don't be late! A Capricorn woman carries herself with an aura of grace and femininity. She may seem a little cool and reserved at first, but she'll lighten up as soon as she feels comfortable around you. There is something dignified about her, but if you look closely, you'll notice a cheeky glint in her eyes. She offers far more than what your first impression might trick you into believing.

Emergency fixes for embarrassing pauses.
She's far too polite to allow embarrassing pauses to occur. If the conversation slows down, she will take the initiative to talk about different topics. However, if this does happen, it probably means the two of you haven't hit it off, and she will probably make an excuse to leave early.

Your place or mine?
Neither. The Capricorn woman is not into casual sex or superficial flings. If you imply any erotic intent during your first date, you may push her away. But don't be fooled into thinking that she's not interested in sex, because she is. She can be very passionate and determined in bed. However, she needs to feel comfortable around her partner before she can fully appreciate the physical sensations.

Checklist, before you dash out to meet her:
Be polished and groomed
(hint: Be classy)
Carry small items of luxury, old or new: a watch, a pen, etc. (hint: Show good taste)
Make sure everything is organized: tickets, table and transport (hint: Pamper her)
Be up-to-date on the arts scene, or something similar (hint: Be interesting)
Have your wallet ready…
(hint: Don't be cheap)

Tip: She appreciates style, quality and a little luxury – but never confuse money with class. A thick gold chain nesting in a hairy chest is (usually) a big no-no!

CHAPTER 1

PREPARE YOURSELF

Catch her eye, capture her attention
Top 10 attention grabbers

1. Be gallant and carry yourself with poise.
2. Show off subtle signs of luxury like nice shoes or a watch (but no flashy bling).
3. Offer your assistance if someone needs it.
4. Take the initiative to invite her out.
5. Be strong and independent, but still attentive and gentle.
6. Let her in on your ideas for the future, but also let her see that you have your feet on the ground.
7. Emphasise some of the things you are good at without bragging.
8. Ask for her opinion and compliment her ideas.
9. Namedropping is fine, provided it fits into the conversation naturally.
10. Maintain a warmth in your expression.

The HE. The man!

You've either got it or you don't. The Capricorn woman will discern very quickly whether you're the type of guy she's looking for. If she's not sure, she will probably give you a second chance. However, there are a few basic requirements. She loves having a man around that makes her feel like a woman. She doesn't mind a good-looking body, but she values intelligence, so you must be able to flex more than just your biceps.

The Essence of him
Stylish and classy – intelligent – well informed, especially about things she can apply to her life (like food, drink and the arts) – independent – ambitious – strong and protective, with a masculine attitude – passionate and sensual – attractive and well-groomed – optimistic – supportive – appreciative of the good things in life, but not prone to throw money around

Capricorn arousal meter
From 0 to 100... Fifteen minutes. There's a time and place for everything. If the setting is right, she will warm up to your erotic advances very quickly.

Remember: Be true to yourself
It doesn't matter if she is the most stunning girl you've ever met – if you don't match, you don't match. You may be able to put on a show for a while to hold her attention, but what's the point? We can't please everybody. We all have different needs, dreams, tastes and preferences. There's no such thing as a one-size-fits-all lover. Be yourself, and be true to who you are – always!

Very important: The Capricorn woman values quality in every area of life. Make sure you are genuine in everything you do. Be stylish. Be charming. Be strong.

CHAPTER 2

THE FIRST DATE

Getting your foot in the door
The basics

Don't get too personal. A casual 'Tell me about yourself' won't work. The Capricorn woman will not reveal her thoughts and feelings to someone she doesn't know.

Patience pays off. Her attitude can cause some men to regard her as out-of-reach, but that's not the case. It just takes a little patience.

No erotic advances. She is cool, controlled and not keen on casual sex – no matter how dishy the guy might be.

Smooth and classy. Be a gentleman. She's not attracted to showoffs or people who throw money around.

Be informed. Take a genuine interest in what goes on in the world. Read a couple of books or visit an art exhibition before seeing her – or at least check out reviews on the internet.

No showing off. Don't be superficial or pretend to know more about something than you do. She will call your bluff.

Give her a small gift, preferably a little luxury.

Whatever you do...

- **DON'T** come across as cheap. Treat her to something nice.

- **DON'T** brag about your job, your car or whatever.

- **DON'T** criticize independent women.

- **DON'T** be rude to the waiter or to people around you.

- **DON'T** forget your manners. Be polite and attentive.

Remember,
If she thinks she's been wrong about you, she will disappear quickly.

- **DON'T** ask her about personal or sensitive issues if you've just met.

- **DON'T** start a discussion just for the sake of it.

- **DON'T** expect her to split the check.

- **DON'T** suggest having sex on the first date.

- **DON'T** be late or forget to call her the next day.

Never get too comfortable and take her attention for granted. Keep being charming!

Signs you're in - or not

This woman will actually let you know that she likes you. She may not walk up to you and say 'Hey!', but she will make it clear through her attitude and her actions that you have captured her interest and eventually her heart. She is persistent in every area of her life, including romance and sensuality. She believes that anything worth having is worth fighting for, and if you have captured her heart – she will make an effort to keep you in her life. Although the signs are usually quite clear, you may also want to keep an eye out for the following:

Chances are she will…

- show up at a function that she knows you will be attending, looking stunning
- make an effort to dazzle you with her looks and femininity
- casually give you a small – but expensive! – gift
- offer to help you with something
- emphasise her admiration for you
- take the initiative to call and text you

Not your type? Making an exit

The Capricorn woman is patient, a true 'stayer'. If she feels that a man is worth the effort, she will wait, work and try to sort things out. She may even get quite stubborn about it. This stubbornness can result from a mixture of hurt feelings and hurt pride. Having to admit that she failed in a relationship – as well as having her heart crushed – can be too much to handle. In these situations, she will try to find reasons to stay, and she will try to convince her partner to stay as well.

If you're not interested in keeping the relationship going, and if you know that happiness waits for both of you elsewhere, you may have to be blunt. Don't give her any cause to misinterpret your actions. Be perfectly clear about what you're doing, and make her realise that choosing you was a mistake.

Foolproof exit measures:

Before you go ahead with any of these suggestions, be prepared to look like an idiot. She will probably get mad and tell you to get a grip before she dumps you.

- Give her a cheap gift that you picked up at a gas station
- Meet her for a date unshaven and wearing dirty clothes
- Forget to bring your wallet and make her pay for the date
- Get overly emotional about everything
- Tell her that you are thinking about giving up your job and becoming a poet
- Show little or no interest in sex – unless it's in a public restroom or in the backseat of your car

CHAPTER 3

SEX'N STUFF

Seductive moves:
How to get her in the mood:

This is actually quite easy. The Capricorn woman enjoys frequent sex and doesn't mind taking the lead. However, she will also appreciate the initiative coming from her man. She doesn't need long-lasting foreplay. The erotic sparks fly freely and quickly from her, and she is usually ready to enjoy her partner in no time.

Preferences and erotic nature

She is attracted to strong, cultivated, polite and stylish men. A man who manages to reveal a physical interest simply by looking at her will also make her heart beat faster. As soon as you have won her trust and affection, turning her on will be easy – she will actually expect you to. If you can show your affection through a seductive smile and a gentle kiss, she will probably respond in kind. A lazy partner will not remain in her life for long. She enjoys being erotically assertive and may start undressing you when she feels the mood coming on, and then it won't take long before she has seduced you completely...

Hitting the right buttons

Although every sign has areas on the body that are more sensitive than others, individual sensitivity may vary quite a bit. Don't go body-blind. Honing in on these erogenous zones and forgetting the rest of her is not a good idea. Use these areas to create sparks while turning her on, and as a passion-booster when things get heated. Watch her body language – including the most obvious of signs. Open your mind to the sensuality of touch and taste.

Key areas
Her back and stomach

Get it on
The Capricorn woman is sensual and erotic, a dream to turn on. Pay attention to her lower back, and you will get results very quickly. Light touches, soft kisses and even a gentle massage will make her tingle inside...

Arouse her
The possibilities for arousing her are almost endless. Two areas in particular that will respond extremely well to kisses and gentle nibbles are the tender skin around her navel and the backs of her knees. These can be described as magic spots. If she seems reluctant to have sex, a gentle flicker with your tongue in these areas may change all that.

Surprise her
Treat her to a private show. She enjoys undressing her partner, but this time, only allow her to watch. Be seductive, be erotic and tease her until she simply has to touch you.

Spice it up
Although she's not into elaborate foreplay, whipped cream or a touch of honey around her navel followed by a playful tongue can add a passionate dimension to make the sex even more intense.

Remember: Although she is passionate and erotic, she prefers to have sex in comfortable surroundings. Never suggest anywhere out of the ordinary.

Her expectations

Exploring the flavours of the main course. No need to worry if you're not a foreplay expert. She doesn't mind moving onto the real thing more or less right away.

Takes the initiative. She enjoys being assertive in bed and often initiates sex.

Stick to the menu. Don't introduce any erotic surprises while having sex. She prefers to know what to expect.

No erotic circus. Erotic gymnastics are not her style. She prefers the traditional pleasures of sex.

Sensual enthusiasm. She is passionate and enthusiastic, and she always manages to turn traditional positions into something new and exciting.

Bring out the passion. She expects passion and sensual enthusiasm from her partner.

Pace yourself. Never push her. She enjoys exploring sex at her own pace. If you really need her to move on, let her know gently.

Visual stimulus. Watching her partner undress slowly and seductively, can create sudden erotics sparks.

Your sensual preferences
Quiz yourself and find out whether this woman is for you.

Where on the scale are you?
1 = Don't agree | 3 = Sure | 5 = Agree!

1. Passion is very important for a fulfilling sex life.
One a scale for 1 to 5, you are: 1 - 2 - 3- 4 - 5

2. Frequent sex makes a relationship more energetic and inspiring.
One a scale for 1 to 5, you are: 1 - 2 - 3- 4 - 5

3. Being undressed or undressing someone else can be very arousing in itself.
One a scale for 1 to 5, you are: 1 - 2 - 3- 4 - 5

4. Sex can be fulfilling even without sex toys or new positions.
One a scale for 1 to 5, you are: 1 - 2 - 3- 4 - 5

Score.
15 - 20: You are passionate, erotic and well matched to her.
10 - 14: She may take you by surprise a couple of times, but her passion and assertiveness thrill you.
05 - 09: She may be a little too much for you at times, but other times, you wish she could be more adventurous. Communicate your needs.
01 - 04: Both of you may broaden your horizons if you listen and learn from each other.

CHAPTER 4

GENERAL STUFF

The big picture

Keep in mind that the characteristics of a Capricorn may vary quite a bit depending on where within the sign she was born, as well as a wide range of additional astrological factors. But for now, let's stick to the basics. Just remember: don't jump to conclusions as soon as you meet her. Give her room to shine. Get to know the woman behind the sign.

Her personality: Pros and cons

Pros
- Persistent
- Independent
- Feminine
- Stylish
- Passionate
- Neat and organised
- Affectionate
- A perfectionist
- Reliable and loyal
- Intelligent
- Passionate
- Ambitious
- Optimistic
- Efficient

Cons
- Snobbish
- Stubborn
- Superficial
- A loner
- Pushy
- Reserved
- Cautious
- Afraid of showing weakness
- Afraid of not measuring up
- Afraid of losing control
- Ruthless
- Arrogant
- Self-centred
- Suppresses her feelings

Tip: How to show romantic interest

Old-fashioned attentiveness, generosity and style will always capture her attention. Masculinity is important to her. She is independent and needs a strong man around her.

Romantic Vibes

Miss Capricorn: The strong and tender partner

The essence

Committed. In her opinion, either you're in a relationship with her or you're not. She knows that a relationship takes commitment, which is why she seldom rushes into things.

Tempted by comfort. Sometimes, she makes choices based on practical preferences rather than her feelings. This can result in short-lived relationships.

Be present, be supportive. Intimacy means a lot to her, and receiving support and encouragement from her man is very important.

Masculinity rules. When it comes to feeling comfortable on an emotional level, she needs a strong and caring man by her side. Although she is independent, she longs for security and protection.

Loyal. When she finally finds the man who satisfies her emotional and practical needs, she will stick with him no matter what happens.

Putting her foot down! Although she is loyal, she is no pushover. She expects the feelings and commitment to be mutual. She may not leave if there's a problem, but she will put her foot down and give her partner a piece of her mind.

Tip: How to show erotic interest

Don't try seducing her if you've only just met her. She needs to feel comfortable around a guy before she beds him. If you do know her, be masculine in your approach. Drop a gentle hint, and use your voice and your eyes to seduce her.

Erotic Vibrations

Miss Capricorn:
The cool and hot lover

The essence

Ease into it. There will be no immediate passion. She takes pride in being cool and controlled.

...or dive in. She will respond quickly to hints and suggestions – provided that she's close to the man and feels comfortable around him. At that point, she will give herself completely and become a passionate partner.

Hot and passionate. She has a strong sex drive and enjoys having sex frequently.

Comfort is a must. In her opinion, sex belongs in the comfort of the bedroom – or at least inside, in a private setting. Don't suggest a quick one in the backseat of your car; you will only be told off.

Don't get kinky. She prefers the traditional and comfortable aspects of sex.

Bring on the main course. As soon as she feels passionate, she will keep going for a long time. Endurance and persistence are her trademark in every aspect of life.

Stamina. She expects her partner to keep it up. A guy who goes to sleep after fifteen minutes of passionate sex will be kicked out of her bed.

CHAPTER 5

COMPATIBILITY QUIZ

Are you banging your head against the wall, or does she unleash your positive potential? Do you provoke her or bring out the best in her? Is she making you throw your arms into the air in exasperation, or do you feel inspired and complete in her company? Take the test to find out.

Question 1
Do you think it's important to be persistent until you have reached your goal?

A. That depends on the goal. Some things are worth fighting for.
B. Of course it's important. How else are you going to succeed?
C. Perhaps, but I'm not that patient.

Question 2.
Do you feel comfortable with traditional sex?

A. It strikes me as quite boring.
B. It's OK, provided I can introduce variations to the old themes every now and then.
C. Yes! Comfortable sex doesn't have to be boring. It can be very passionate.

(cont.)

Question 3.
Do you prefer having sex in unusual places or in private and comfortable surroundings?

A. I prefer sex in comfortable surroundings – and preferably with a bottle of wine.
B. I get a kick out of having sex in unusual places. Traditional routines aren't my thing.
C. I prefer safer and more comfortable surroundings – although I do find the idea of sex on a beach very exciting.

Question 4.
Do you show your romantic feelings?

A. I usually forget, but I'm sure she knows how I feel about her.
B. Reassurance is important for a happy relationship. I regularly tell my girlfriend that I love her.
C. Sometimes I do, sometimes I don't. It depends on the mood.

Question 5.
What kind of woman turns you on?

A. The healthy, outdoorsy type.
B. The playful and girlish type.
C. The stylish, cool and passionate type.

Question 6.
How would you describe yourself?

A. Focused, conservative and serious.
B. Cool, ambitious and wise.
C. Reserved, caring and intelligent.

Question 7.
If you were struggling with a problem, would you tell your partner?

A. Of course. If I can't trust my girlfriend, who can I trust?
B. No, I'm too proud. I prefer to sort things out on my own.
C. I suppose I would tell her, but it depends on what it was about.

Question 8.
Do you think it's possible to express love through sex?

A. I guess ... I don't really think about it.
B. Absolutely! If you cannot express love when you're having sex, you're not on the same level as each other.
C. Sex and love are two different things. Why try to mix them?

Question 9.
You are going away for a week. Would you suggest phone sex?

A. Never – that seems vulgar.
B. Of course! Sex over the phone is good fun.
C. Perhaps, but only if my girlfriend indicated that she'd like to try it.

Question 10.
What kind of foreplay do you prefer?

A. Romantic and sensual, with champagne and soft music.
B. Short and passionate.
C. I'm not too keen on foreplay at all.

SCORE	A	B	C
Question 1	5	10	1
Question 2	1	5	10
Question 3	10	1	5
Question 4	1	10	5
Question 5	5	1	10
Question 6	1	5	10
Question 7	10	5	1
Question 8	5	10	1
Question 9	10	1	5
Question 10	10	5	1

75 – 100
Few worries, if any. Love, affection and passion. Comfort and luxury. This may sound like something from a novel, but when two people who are on the same level manage to find each other, bliss happens. The bond between you will become stronger as time goes by. The support you give each other can provide you with the confidence and enthusiasm you need in order to move onward in your professional lives. A feeling of security makes it feel safe to explore life – together. And your sensual life is just as rewarding. Enjoy!

51 – 74
It seems as though nothing much could possibly go wrong in this relationship. There won't be many arguments – simply because there's not much to argue about. When it comes to sex, you're a rare match. Not many people manage to express love through sex the way you do. Intimacy is a keyword in discussing your relationship. Continue to be the protective man she needs you to be, and the relationship will thrive.

26 – 50
You probably have mixed feelings about this relationship. You respect and admire your partner, but she can be a challenge. She has high expectations, and sometimes you regard them as a little superficial. A nice house and a fancy car aren't everything in life. Maybe you miss the adventure, the unknown and the erotic mysteries – which you never get to explore with her. It's possible that the relationship is moving in a direction that doesn't feel right. Love conquers all – but nothing much happens if you don't communicate and try to solve your differences. The relationship is definitely possible. The question is: Are the two of you interested in pulling together, or will you simply pull apart?

10 – 25
Are things getting a little boring? Nothing new going on in the bedroom? Too much work and no time to play? If the answer is yes, it might be wise to do something about it before the two of you drift apart completely. If the pressure to perform is getting too much to handle, ask her to see you as you are – not as a superhuman. Communication is the first step to understanding each other. Try to approach her in a slightly different way. Give her a little more attention. If the relationship still feels like a hassle, the two of you should consider looking for romance, happiness and sensual fulfilment elsewhere.

Thoughts…
Communication is the key that can open doors. Take time to listen, and listen with an open mind and open heart.

AQUARIUS the female

YOUR DATE: AQUARIUS
20 January – 18 February

The Essence of her

Sensitive – intellectual – impulsive and does things on the spur of the moment – enjoys new activities – loves broadening her horizons – charming – imaginative – stubborn – choosy and waits a long time before entering into a relationship – independent – doesn't mind pursuing hobbies on her own – original – creative – entertaining – manages to discover the positive side of most people – loves having people around

…and remember: She finds men fascinating and usually has quite a few male friends. However, if you have sparked her romantic interest, there's no need to be jealous.

Blind Date – speedy essentials

Who's waiting for you?
The Aquarius woman finds people stimulating and loves places where she can interact with others. She has probably suggested meeting in a lively bar or café. If you're late, or she is early, she will probably already be chatting away with somebody. Remember that for her, a blind date is a chance to get to know someone new. Romance and sensual feelings will come later. She is sparkling and charming, with an alert mind. Men who are looking for a quick catch will be disappointed. She is not into fast fun – unless you actually mean fast fun, like catching a plane somewhere or just doing something out of the ordinary.

Emergency fixes for embarrassing pauses.
Although she can be a little shy, especially if she likes you, there won't be any embarrassing pauses. She has a lot of things to talk about. As soon as you start interacting with her, you'll find her rattling on for hours. If the conversation does become slow and difficult, it probably means you don't have much in common. If this happens, there's no point in dragging it out.

Your place or mine?
Neither. You can use all of your favourite tricks – be funny, interesting and tell her about your amazing massages – but it will get you nowhere. She is neither cold nor difficult to arouse; she simply prefers to wait for that special guy comes around. That doesn't mean she won't hang around with you until the early hours of the morning. If she finds you interesting, she probably will. But don't confuse this with erotic intent.

Checklist, before you dash out to meet her:
Wear something unique (t-shirt, socks)
(hint: Stand out without looking silly)
Have suggestions for what to eat and where to go
(hint: Be creative)
Carry a book or an unusual bag
(hint: A good conversation starter)
Bring a small surprise
(hint: Make it special)
Brush up on an interesting topic
(hint: Be interesting)

Tip: Make sure to set yourself apart with something unusual. Draw her attention with something you wear, something you know or a story about something you've done.

CHAPTER 1

PREPARE YOURSELF

Catch her eye, capture her attention
Top 10 attention grabbers

1. Pay her a compliment for something that others wouldn't have noticed.
2. Show compassion for others and offer your assistance.
3. Don't be afraid to speak out and voice your opinion.
4. Be original and stand out from the crowd.
5. Show creativity, enthusiasm and a positive attitude.
6. Be genuinely interested in her.
7. Introduce her to something new, whether a topic, an exotic spa or an exhibition.
8. Make sure that something about your appearance captures her attention.
9. Suggest trying or making some exotic food.
10. Tell her about something that's on your mind and ask for her opinion.

The HE. The man!

He must be able to appeal to her on many different levels. There must be something special about him – nothing major, just something that makes him stand out from the crowd. The Aquarius woman's perfect partner is an adventurer who can join her in making the days come alive with excitement. He must be independent, but still loyal and trustworthy. He must be a free spirit, but never give her any reason to be jealous. He will be entertaining, inspiring, strong and sensual. And finding him…? No wonder there are so many single Aquarian women.

The Essence of him
Individualistic – creative – adventurous – artistic – entertaining and able to broaden her horizons – a free spirit, but faithful – outgoing – positive and enthusiastic with a fondness for new ideas – independent and confident – open-minded – an erotic explorer who loves sensuality – intelligent with the ability of thinking in new directions – forthcoming and friendly

Aquarius arousal meter
From 0 to 100… Two hours or more. She enjoys exploring sex gradually. She can be spontaneous, but she still takes her time.

Remember: Be true to yourself
It doesn't matter if she is the most stunning girl you've ever met – if you don't match, you don't match. You may be able to put on a show for a while to hold her attention, but what's the point? We can't please everybody. We all have different needs, dreams, tastes and preferences. There's no such thing as a one-size-fits-all lover. Be yourself, and be true to who you are – always!

Very important: You need to appeal to her mind. Be yourself. If you have an original streak, let it show. If you have sparked her mind, her body and heart will follow.

CHAPTER 2

THE FIRST DATE

**Getting your foot in the door
The basics**

Make the first move. Although sparkling and outgoing, the Aquarius woman may be shy about asking a man out on a date – especially if she really likes him.

Make it special. Take her to a special place. This could be a theatre showing an interesting play or a restaurant that specializes in exotic food.

Be personal. Be smart. Be patient. Make sure she gets a glimpse of your private personality. Show her that you are well read, intelligent and take an interest in current affairs.

Entertain and fascinate. Interesting topics will make her pay attention. She expects her date to entertain her and broaden her horizons.

A creative gift. She loves receiving gifts, especially if they are a little out of the ordinary, but not necessarily expensive.

No verbal erotics. Don't start talking about sex right away – unless it's a fascinating topic you'd like to discuss in a conversational way.

Whatever you do...

- **DON'T** be blunt and limit the conversation to sports etc.

- **DON'T** imply that a woman's place is by a man's side.

- **DON'T** be pushy. Ask to see her again, but do it casually.

- **DON'T** emphasize all the things you don't like.

- **DON'T** scan the menu for the cheapest items.

Remember,
Although she is adventurous and independent, she does need balance and trust in

- **DON'T** suggest getting intimate before you are comfortable in each other's company.

- **DON'T** get jealous when she bumps into male friends.

- **DON'T** criticize open-minded people with different views.

- **DON'T** provoke her and get into political discussions.

- **DON'T** act macho.

her life. Never make her feel insecure by flirting with other women.

Signs you're in - or not

This is not easy to figure out. An Aquarius woman gets on with men in general and has a comfortable relationship with many of her friends. She can get really shy if she likes a guy, and this doesn't make it any easier. Don't expect her to be direct about it. She is not assertive, even when she is romantically interested. You'll need to look out for subtle hints. She will loosen up after you have taken the initiative, but when is a good time to take the initiative? There are signs that you may have triggered her interest:

Chances are she will...

- spend more time with you than other friends
- open up, talk about herself and risk being vulnerable
- treat you to something special, like a home-cooked meal
- casually touch you and be close to you
- introduce you to her friends
- call and text you frequently – provided you already took the initiative

Not your type? Making an exit

This would be an unusual scenario. An Aquarius woman takes a long time before she commits to a relationship – and we're not just talking about marriage. Any romantic relationship will have her thinking and pondering for quite some time. She needs to get to know you. She needs to feel that you're on the same level. This is why so many Aquarians remain single for a long periods of time. If the two of you are in a relationship, it will usually mean that you have spent a long time getting to getting to know each other.

But maybe she didn't live up to your expectations. Maybe she's too independent and happy doing things on her own. If you've tried talking to her and still can't get through, it might be time to move on and seek happiness elsewhere. If she's too busy to take a hint, you may need to be a little blunt about it.

Foolproof exit measures:

Before you go ahead with any of these suggestions, be prepared to look like an idiot. She will probably get mad and tell you to get a grip before she dumps you.

- Insist on having sex frequently, passionately and on the spur of the moment
- Criticize her friends and act jealous of her male friends
- Tell her to spend more time at home
- Leave laundry and ironing for her to do
- Spend your time watching TV
- Interrupt her when she's talking and criticize her views

CHAPTER 3

SEX'N STUFF

Seductive moves:
How to get her in the mood:

Many different things turn her on, but the macho approach is not one of them. A tight t-shirt and flexed muscles won't do it for her. She needs to be aroused through imagination and anticipation. Something about her partner must be special enough to trigger her curiosity. A man with exotic, erotic knowledge will always have an advantage...

Preferences and erotic nature

An Aquarius woman gets a kick out of a creative and erotic mind. Intense passion is not that important to her. She wants to become one with her partner and experience sex on a different level. Spirituality is keyword in her sensual life. Being on the same wavelength is a must. She is turned on by the prospect of experiencing new and exciting sexual adventures – provided they are not crude or vulgar. She is also turned on by knowing that she can please her man and bring him to new erotic heights. She is an attentive lover and would never become lazy in bed. There's nothing cynical about her sex life. Everything she does is based in harmony, respect and attention.

Hitting the right buttons

Although every sign has areas on the body that are more sensitive than others, individual sensitivity may vary quite a bit. Don't go body-blind. Honing in on these erogenous zones and forgetting the rest of her is not a good idea. Use these areas to create sparks while turning her on, and as a passion-booster when things get heated. Watch her body language – including the most obvious of signs. Open your mind to the sensuality of touch and taste.

Key areas
Her calves and ankles

Get it on
Pay attention to her calves and ankles. Be creative about it, and you'll discover that there are many ways to arouse her. No matter what you do, be gentle. If your touch is too rough, you'll turn her off.

Arouse her
Practice a bit of harmless foot flirting when you're out. Use as much of your foot and leg as you can to stimulate hers. In private, there are many different ways to play with these sensitive areas. A bath will give you an opportunity to focus on her feet. Follow up with a gentle foot massage, and the erotic temperature will be rising...

Surprise her
Gentle kisses and nibbles around her ankles will make her tingle. Use a bit of honey or whipped cream to make the experience even more sensual. While kissing one leg, gently caress the other. Don't rush it. Take your time.

Spice it up
Warm oil around her ankles and a gentle massage may seem innocent, but this can spark the passion in her. The temperature will make the sensation more intense. Apply it generously and let your fingers slide gently over her ankles.

Remember: Never be blunt when trying to seduce her. Take it slow and appeal to her imagination. A slightly erotic visual – nothing graphic! – may spark her imagination.

Her expectations

Go exploring. She is a warm and exciting lover who enjoys exploring the mysteries of sex.

Let the creativity flow. You will soon discover that she is very imaginative – more than the average woman.

Try something new. Doing the same routine over and over again bores her. She will persuade her partner to try new things, or different variations of traditional positions.

Touch her gently. She enjoys caressing her partner's body, preferably when he is caressing hers at the same time.

A sassy whisper. She appreciates a man who stimulates her mind by whispering erotic words into her ear during sex. This can bring out the playfulness in her.

Playful suggestions. Her sexual philosophy is: 'What pleases him pleases me.' This means that she enjoys a wide variety of activities, provided they're not too crude or kinky.

If it's good, let her know. It's very important to her that her partner clearly expresses his enjoyment of what she's doing.

Share your fantasies. She is very open-minded and appreciates a partner who talks about his fantasies.

Your sensual preferences
Quiz yourself and find out whether this woman is for you.

Where on the scale are you?
1 = Don't agree | 3 = Sure | 5 = Agree!

1. Exploring the nuances of sex is more important than a quick climax.
One a scale for 1 to 5, you are: 1 - 2 - 3- 4 - 5

2. Communication through touch and whispers is important during sex.
One a scale for 1 to 5, you are: 1 - 2 - 3- 4 - 5

3. It's important that a woman participates actively during sex.
One a scale for 1 to 5, you are: 1 - 2 - 3- 4 - 5

4. Foreplay is important and starts before the clothes come off.
One a scale for 1 to 5, you are: 1 - 2 - 3- 4 - 5

Score.
15 - 20: This will never be boring. You both appreciate new experiences, closeness and playful pleasures ... enjoy!
10 - 14: She may take you by surprise at times, but this will only make the erotic experience more exciting.
05 - 09: Sometimes you just want to make it quick and passionate. Let her know how you feel.
01 - 04: She's either too demanding, or you are too passionate. Communication is the key to enjoyment.

CHAPTER 4

GENERAL STUFF

The big picture

Keep in mind that the characteristics of an Aquarius may vary quite a bit depending on where within the sign she was born, as well as a wide range of additional astrological factors. But for now, let's stick to the basics. Just remember: don't jump to conclusions as soon as you meet her. Give her room to shine. Get to know the woman behind the sign.

Her personality: Pros and cons

Pros
- Sparkling
- Friendly
- Adventurous
- Outgoing
- Kind
- Understanding
- Independent
- Creative
- Curious
- Original
- Not afraid to start over
- Enthusiastic
- Supportive
- An erotic explorer

Cons
- Emotionally detached
- Restless
- Indecisive about love
- Self-centred
- A slow starter erotically
- Ignores her feelings
- Naïve
- Prone to drift
- Indecisive
- Insecure
- Insensitive to other's feelings
- Impractical
- Self-pitying
- Emotionally ignorant

Tip: How to show romantic interest

Take her to a gathering or event that relates to something she is interested in. She needs to feel mentally connected with her partner, and this is a good place to start.

Romantic Vibes

Miss Aquarius:
The enthusiastic and feminine partner

The essence

The friend-zone. Everything starts with friendship, and the friendship will continue even when things get a little more intimate and romantic. The challenge is the transition from friendship to romance. If you don't manage to spark her romantic interest, you'll remain in the 'friends' zone.

Independent. She is an independent partner and doesn't mind pursuing her own interests.

Absentminded. There are always things running through her mind and may come across as a little distracted and emotionally distant sometimes. It's not her intention to withhold her feelings; she just assumes her partner knows.

No mind-reader. She may be unaware of her partner's emotional needs unless he tells her. Her emotional antennas are not particularly well tuned.

Share her energy. She is positive and sparkling and will approach a relationship with enthusiasm – provided that her partner shares her optimism. A slow and unimaginative man will drain her energy and make her feel miserable.

Quality time. She loves having people around, but she also values intimacy – both mental and sensual – with her partner.

Tip: How to show erotic interest

Be creative about it. Casually ask her about exotic sensuality, such as tantric sex, and whether it's just a fad or actually something that can increase sensual pleasure.

Erotic Vibrations

Miss Aquarius:
The adventurous and considerate lover

The essence

Gentle in her ways. There is nothing aggressive about her – she may be assertive, but never pushy.

Understanding. She takes great pride in pleasing her partner. As part of this, she is very understanding. If things are moving slowly, she will patiently arouse her partner until he is roaring to go.

Erotic explorer. Adventure is important to her, and she will explore new variations of old themes in order to keep her sex life fresh and exciting.

Sensual firework. Although she may come across as a slow mover, there's nothing slow about her. She will turn out to be a firework of sexual pleasures.

Erotic spice. When she's in the right mood, she is eager to try out different ideas. She is very imaginative and has a unique ability to brighten things up with erotic spice.

Intimacy means a lot to her. Caresses and gentle touches are paramount for her to achieve sensual pleasure.

Mutual pleasure. Pleasing her partner is just as important to her as pleasing herself – sometimes even more so. Paying close attention to her partner's needs comes naturally to her.

CHAPTER 5

COMPATIBILITY QUIZ

Are you banging your head against the wall, or does she unleash your positive potential? Do you provoke her or bring out the best in her? Is she making you throw your arms into the air in exasperation, or do you feel inspired and complete in her company? Take the test to find out.

Question 1
Have you ever toyed with the idea of trying erotic activities that are a little out of the ordinary?

A. Well, I do have fantasies, but I tend to leave them at that.
B. No, I prefer to keep it safe and comfortable!
C. Yes, several times. I have even tried tantric sex – it's very satisfying.

Question 2
During sex, your partner suddenly stops what she's doing and starts telling you about something exciting that happened to her earlier that day. Well..?

A. I guess that's my cue to sleep.
B. I would probably forget about the sex. My partner is engaging and entertaining, and I always get a kick out of listening to her.
C. Typical. I would laugh and hit her over the head with a pillow.

(cont.)

Question 3.
You wake up one morning feeling really hot. How do you react when your partner ignores you and starts telling you about her plans for the day?

A. No big deal. I can be pretty enthusiastic myself.
B. I would just pull the blanket over my head and 'sort things out' on my own.
C. My immediate reply would be: Fine, but make sure to wear something sassy when you get back…

Question 4.
Your 'toolbox' is not functioning properly one evening. What would you prefer your partner to do?

A. Focusing on herself while keeping an eye on me.
B. Nothing. Just leave me alone.
C. Show affection, play around with my tools a little bit and see what happens.

Question 5.
Would it surprise you if your partner asked you to tell her about your previous sexual experiences?

A. Not at all. Sharing sexual history is an important part of developing a healthy sex life.
B. Maybe. It would probably make me a little shy.
C. My previous sexual experiences are nobody's business.

Question 6.
Are you adaptable?

A. Not really.
B. Yes. I have a great time anywhere I go.
C. Yes, but reluctantly.

Question 7.
Does it bother you that your partner doesn't seem particularly dependent on you?

A. Not at all. In fact, it makes me feel good. I'm glad she's independent.
B. Yes. it's my biggest worry. I'm quite jealous.
C. I've got mixed feelings. I'm glad she's independent, but I want to be a part of her life, and to have a voice in her life.

Question 8.
Do you sometimes get the impression that your partner is more interested in your mind than your body?

A. Yes – and although I know I should take it as a compliment, it can make me feel a little annoyed.
B. Mind and body? They're the same thing, aren't they?
C. She likes me. That's good enough for me.

Question 9.
Have you ever got so carried away during foreplay that you forgot about an orgasm?

A. No! That's impossible.
B. Once or twice, and only when I've been in a playful mood.
C. Several times. Sex is much more than just orgasms.

Question 10.
Are you impulsive?

A. Yes, very. My friends tell me I'm a little too impulsive at times.
B. No, I firmly believe in making plans!
C. Sometimes, if I'm not busy.

SCORE	A	B	C
Question 1	5	1	10
Question 2	1	10	5
Question 3	10	5	1
Question 4	5	1	10
Question 5	10	5	1
Question 6	1	10	5
Question 7	10	1	5
Question 8	5	10	1
Question 9	1	5	10
Question 10	10	1	5

75 – 100
Do you ever find time to go out and visit your friends? Chances are that the two of you enjoy each other's company so much that you tend to get absorbed in your collective adventures, ideas and anything that can broaden your horizons. You have discovered a new energy in life, which you apply in every context– including sex. Every day holds something new for you to explore. Stick with her and you will never be bored.

51 – 74
Make sure to be open and communicative, and there won't be many bumps in the road. She is a free spirit – but this inspires you more than it bothers you. It's liberating to have a woman around who wakes up every morning and embraces the world. She makes you dream and feel alive. In return, you give her the strength and security she longs for – even if she doesn't admit it. Sensuality brings you together and allows you to connect on different levels. Nurture this relationship.

26 – 50

Are you out of breath? Slow down for a second and think. Are you attracted to the adventures, or are you attracted to the woman? She is impulsive and brings out the energy in you, but does she make you feel alive or worn out? In order to get the most out of this relationship, you need to figure out whether she satisfies your basic needs. If she doesn't, it won't last forever. If she does, it might be a good idea to communicate n order to avoid misunderstandings. Try being a bit more flexible and adaptable. This will make her feel more relaxed. And if you want to change something, tell her. She is no mind-reader.

10 – 25

Things could probably be a lot better. Why are you sticking Have you ever tried to capture a butterfly without damaging its wings? Whenever you want to discuss something important or experience a passionate moment, she is usually off somewhere on her own. This is not the basis for your perfect relationship. Although she's entertaining and interesting, there's something missing. Life feels hurried and superficial. There's never time for any depth. Unless you are on the same level, it will be difficult to make her understand and adjust. Happiness and fulfillment wait elsewhere – for both of you.

Thoughts...
It's love, not a partner quiz, that determines the future of your relationship.

PISCES the female

YOUR DATE: PISCES
19 February–20 March

The Essence of her

Feminine – sweet, with an innocent attitude – lively, sparkling and socially active – tolerant and liberal – sensitive – slightly insecure – sensual and erotically assertive – kind, caring and understanding – extremely positive with a constructive outlook on life – a dreamer; easily inspired – creative – prone to escapism – an incurable romantic

...and remember: Flexibility and mutual understanding are very important. If she feels cornered, she will simply disappear into her dream world.

Blind Date – speedy essentials

Who's waiting for you?
She might be a little early, simply because she doesn't like being stressed before a date. You'll notice her right away… the smile, the sparkling laughter and the enthusiasm in her eyes. Although she may be talking to other men in the room as you arrive, she'll focus on you for the entire evening. Her femininity is not based on fancy clothes. She will keep it casual and comfortable. There's nothing snobbish about her. Luxurious brands are not important – if it looks good, it's fine.

Emergency fixes for embarrassing pauses.
A Pisces woman will make sure to keep the conversation going, especially if she suspects you are feeling nervous. Her conversation will be bubbly and casual. She won't delve into deep topics right away. She wants to get to know you and your personality. Should the conversation need a slight boost, talk about something unusual you've done or an exotic place you've visited.

Your place or mine?
Location doesn't matter, provided it's comfortable and convenient. She doesn't go on blind dates looking for casual sex –but if you've managed to capture her attention, she will be open to it. An invitation to 'continue the night somewhere else' should be casual, without direct implications of anything erotic. If she joins you, it's because she's noticed something special about you – and not just your toolbox.

Checklist, before you dash out to meet her:
Text her the night before
(hint: Let her know you're excited)
Have ideas about an activity
(hint: Make it special: skydiving, etc.)
Wear simple and masculine attire
(hint: No polkadots or fancy pants)
Be close-shaved or have a groomed beard
(hint: Be well kept)
Prepare a few wine and food suggestions
(hint: But don't be a showoff)

Tip: The Pisces woman is one of the biggest surprises of the zodiac. She may be sparkling, feminine and a little girlish, but she has a sixth sense when it comes to pleasing men – both inside and outside of the bedroom.

CHAPTER 1

PREPARE YOURSELF

Catch her eye, capture her attention
Top 10 attention grabbers

1. A warm smile and a cheerful laugh.
2. Be charming, polite and confident.
3. Introduce her to something unusual that you're knowledgeable about.
4. Present her with a challenge you need solved.
5. Let her know you're a wizard in the kitchen – even if you can only make pizza.
6. Suggest a sporty outdoor activity, preferably something a little unusual.
7. Show compassion; offer a helping hand to strangers.
8. Notice the beauty around you: a nice sunset, falling leaves, etc.
9. Show your sensual side by enjoying your food and drink slowly.
10. Take her dancing.

The HE. The man!

Her ideal man probably lives on different planet – in any case, it's a tall order to find him on this one. Her expectations are high and sometimes unrealistic. However, she keeps searching, and she falls in love frequently. She needs a strong man: someone who makes her feel safe and protected from the world. He must also be sensitive, generous and adventurous. Being an attentive lover goes without saying. 'Earth to Pisces ... please come in. Repeating, Earth to Pisces!'

The Essence of him
Tough and masculine– sensitive and understanding – adventurous – enjoys physical pursuits, preferably outdoors, but also cherishes cosy evenings at home – supportive of his partner professionally and protective of her emotionally – provides her with intimacy, comfort and security – understanding and kind – has an excellent sense of humour – erotically confident and playful

---

Pisces arousal meter
From 0 to 100... In 30 minutes – or three hours. Either she's ready for an erotic encounter, or she's not. Remember, she is sensitive and easily influenced by moods and atmospheres.

Remember: Be true to yourself
It doesn't matter if she is the most stunning girl you've ever met – if you don't match, you don't match. You may be able to put on a show for a while to hold her attention, but what's the point? We can't please everybody. We all have different needs, dreams, tastes and preferences. There's no such thing as a one-size-fits-all lover. Be yourself, and be true to who you are – always!

Very important: Never take a Pisces woman for granted. Let her know you appreciate everything she does for you – including during your more sensual moments.

CHAPTER 2

THE FIRST DATE

Getting your foot in the door
The basics

Let's talk about it. Be open about your problems. She is one of the most caring signs in the zodiac and will always be willing to help you.

Be reliable. A Pisces woman needs to feel secure, and a guy who only shows up when he feels like it will make her miserable. Show her that you are reliable. Being able to trust a man is important to her.

Tough cookie. Don't be fooled by her seemingly innocent or helpless personality; this woman is capable of punching your teeth in – at least metaphorically – when provoked.

Competition. Make a move. If she receives attention from another interesting male, she may leave you out in the cold.

Full package. Although she prefers masculinity and strength, she also values and respects a man's sensitive and romantic side. What she's really looking for is the whole package.

Genuine admiration. Let her know how you feel about her. Admire her looks, her ambition, her commitment... the lot.

Whatever you do...

- **DON'T** be slow to accept her suggestions.

- **DON'T** leave all of the decisions to her. Don't be indecisive.

- **DON'T** give her any reason to doubt you.

- **DON'T** expect frequent sex without commitment.

- **DON'T** try to save her feelings by telling white lies.

Remember, It's important for her to establish a emotional connection with her man.

- **DON'T** be lazy or physically inactive.

- **DON'T** tout blunt or populist views.

- **DON'T** give the impression of being a free spirit who has no intention of settling down.

- **DON'T** brag about your romantic or erotic adventures.

- **DON'T** be cheap. Act generously, and pamper her.

before she can relax and feel comfortable in the relationship.

Signs you're in - or not

The Pisces woman may not be a romantic, but she's in love with love – or at least her perception of love. Although she comes across as sweet and innocent, she is a smart woman who applies her femininity naturally. When you're on a date, she listens, understands, shows interest and smiles while gently touching your hand... You think 'Wow' and put your arms around her. However, she seems to be this friendly with everybody. How do you make sure it's you she's interested in? Pay attention to the following:

Chances are she will...

- invite you to her home or somewhere similarly intimate
- organise activities with friends and include you
- compliment you for being a Man
- seem carried away by your attention
- respond to your texts – quickly!
- appreciate your physical attention: hugs, touches and gentle kisses

Not your type? Making an exit

This woman believes in love – and she believes in miracles, too. If she feels you may have a problem, she'll be right there by your side, helping you to resolve it. If she has a problem? There's always chocolate and a bottle of wine. If the relationship is struggling, she'll want to fix it. How difficult it is to leave her depends on how long you've been together, how well she knows you – and whether she really loves you. If she does, she'll have convinced herself that you have a few things that need sorting out. If these are a few things you don't want to sort out, it might be a good idea to stop the initiative before it starts. Remember, she is sensitive. It might be a very good idea to have a casual chat or two before getting blunt about it.

Foolproof exit measures:

To most people, these actions may seem like nothing more than a hassle – but to the female Pisces, it's serious stuff – and hurtful. Make sure you know what you want before you go ahead with it.

- Insist on being passive during sex
- When you open a gift from her, sigh and say, 'Oh well, it's the thought that counts'
- Criticise her family and friends
- Always choose the cheapest option, no matter what you're doing
- Keep in touch with female friends and ex-girlfriends
- Be indecisive about most things and never let her know where you stand

CHAPTER 3

SEX'N STUFF

Seductive moves:
How to get her in the mood:

If she's in the right frame of mind, it won't take much. Even the smallest hint about sex can funnel her thoughts toward it. It's not that she has a dirty mind – merely fine-tuned sensual antennas. The fact that she may even interpret innocent suggestions erotically just adds a bit of spice to her personality.

Preferences and erotic nature

A seductive look, a sensual touch, a kiss that lasts a moment longer than expected: subtle hints, which other women in the zodiac probably wouldn't even notice, make her shiver with anticipation. She's very receptive to visual stimulation, no matter how innocent. Watching a chick flick with a few erotic scenes is enough to make her hot – and slightly embarrassed, if you've only just met each other. She is easily turned on. However, a man who expects sex without the fun of seduction turns her off. She is sensitive to people taking her for granted, and this applies to an erotic partner as well – maybe even more so.

Hitting the right buttons

Although every sign has areas on the body that are more sensitive than others, individual sensitivity may vary quite a bit. Don't go body-blind. Honing in on these erogenous zones and forgetting the rest of her is not a good idea. Use these areas to create sparks while turning her on, and as a passion-booster when things get heated. Watch her body language – including the most obvious of signs. Open your mind to the sensuality of touch and taste.

Key areas
Her feet

Get it on
You will notice that her feet are pretty, regardless of whether she's wearing nail varnish or not. Pisces women seem to be blessed with beautiful feet that are soft, pleasant and smooth– and very sensitive to sensual attention.

Arouse her
Now, this is a little tricky. Men's feet seldom make the list of their most attractive features – at least not according to most women. That's why playing footsies can be risky. However, if you have well-kept feet to show off, go ahead and gently brush them over hers. Remember to pay attention to her feet during sex as well. Gentle kisses can produce serious sparks.

Surprise her

While watching TV, give her a nice foot massage with some lotion or oil. Whereas other women might fall asleep, the Pisces woman will wake up. Take your time, be gentle and allow her to get into it.

Spice it up

Let her use her feet to touch and caress you. Use plenty of oil and let her play. Be creative about it...

Remember: The Pisces woman enjoys a masculine partner in bed. Be sensitive to her needs, but don't ask how she feels every two minutes.

Her expectations

Making waves. If she could, the Pisces woman would prefer to make love on a waterbed. She finds the movements created by water to be stimulating, seductive and highly erotic.

Masculine vibes. Although her sex drive is strong and her passion intense, she doesn't enjoy taking command in bed. She usually feels more comfortable with a strong partner.

Close the window. If she's stimulated in the right way, she may turn out be a loud lover, inclined to thoroughly express her pleasure. It might be a good idea to close the window before you get started.

Close attention... One of her favourite ways of arousing her partner is to kiss and suck him all over. This demands an awful lot of patience – and she loves it.

Bring on the fantasies. Erotic daydreams are the spice of her sensual life, and she doesn't mind trying out a few fantasies. However, in order to fully enjoy the adventure, she needs a partner who's just as excited as she is.

Your sensual preferences
Quiz yourself and find out whether this woman is for you.

Where on the scale are you?
1 = Don't agree | 3 = Sure | 5 = Agree!

1. Intensity, passion and creativity make for a good erotic cocktail.
One a scale for 1 to 5, you are: 1 - 2 - 3- 4 - 5

2. Too much talk and reassurance can rob sex of some of its impulsiveness.
One a scale for 1 to 5, you are: 1 - 2 - 3- 4 - 5

3. A sensual erotic life is more important than frequent sex.
One a scale for 1 to 5, you are: 1 - 2 - 3- 4 - 5

4. Expressiveness is important during sex.
One a scale for 1 to 5, you are: 1 - 2 - 3- 4 - 5

Score.
15 - 20: Sex is not only frequent, but also sensual, passionate and highly erotic. Enjoy!
10 - 14: She may surprise you from time to time by transforming from a sweet and innocent girl to a sassy and confident babe. The variety will spice up your erotic life.
05 - 09: Never overlook her little hints. Don't take away the magic by asking questions – just gently play along. Her suggestions can make the days very sensual. Take time to enjoy and explore it.
01 - 04: Either she's too much for you, or you are too fixed in your ways. Maybe the two of you are simply misinterpreting each other. Try communicating more.

CHAPTER 4

GENERAL STUFF

The big picture

Keep in mind that the characteristics of a Pisces may vary quite a bit depending on where within the sign she was born, as well as a wide range of additional astrological factors. But for now, let's stick to the basics. Just remember: don't jump to conclusions as soon as you meet her. Give her room to shine. Get to know the woman behind the sign.

Her personality: Pros and cons

Pros
- Feminine and bubbly
- Romantic
- Sensitive
- Compassionate
- Charming and social
- Understanding
- Passionate and sensual
- Uniquely optimistic
- Gets on with different people
- Loyal and supportive
- Energetic
- Has an appetite for life
- Open-minded
- Affectionate

Cons
- Naïve
- Seldom satisfied or fulfilled
- Irrational
- Changes partners – often
- Dates the wrong men – often
- Emotional; a dreamer
- Tries to 'save' men
- Easily hurt and offended
- Prone to escapism
- Overindulgent; sex, food etc
- Overly flirty
- Conflict-averse
- Too eager to please
- Insecure

Tip: How to show romantic interest

Be a tad old-fashioned about it. Show your masculinity and woo her. Invite her out, offer to help her with a practical task, bring a small gift or a flower... Chivalry is a good approach. She will appreciate it.

Romantic Vibes

Miss Pisces:
The romantic and supportive partner

The essence

Dreamy. She is incredibly idealistic – not when it comes to love, but when it comes to men. When she finally finds someone who's on her level, she will be attentive, supportive and loyal.

Constructive compassion. She's fascinated by a guy with a story. Throw in a personal challenge, and she'll be captivated. Her amazingly positive attitude makes her believe she can turn him around and make him happy. Well, reality tends to kick in after a while, and she'll be off on her next adventure.

Security. Although she is perfectly capable of taking care of herself, she longs for a strong man to keep her safe. The Pisces woman tends to settle down with someone who can provide comfort and security – but even so, she craves romance.

A soulmate. She needs a man who sees the same colours as she does – in every aspect of life. She needs to feel alive – and to live!

Make it real. She's not just a dreamer; she actually pursues her romantic dreams, and she wants her man to join her.

Harmony. She will strive to make life comfortable in every way. A Pisces' home is a happy one.

Tip: How to show erotic interest

You don't have to work hard at this. She is very sensitive to erotic suggestions, or even suggestions that she may interpret as erotic. Give her something to wonder about, something that may be erotic ... or maybe not. Tease her a little.

Erotic Vibrations

Miss Pisces:
The warm and tender lover

The essence

Sassy intuition. The Pisces woman seems to have a sixth sense when it comes to doing the right things to get her partner in the mood for sex.

Fun and frisky. She is ultra-feminine, but also determined and passionate. Although she may strike you as soft and maybe even a little timid, she can be a wild thing in bed.

Creative input. Suggestions will be received with enthusiasm – provided they don't offend her sensitive nature.

Genuine. She is tolerant, liberal and patient – a brilliant combination! There's nothing pretentiously cool about her. She is genuinely enthusiastic and easily aroused. A quick look through a dirty magazine is usually all it takes to get her started.

Hot! ...or not! For her, there's no such thing as being mildly interested. Either she's turned on or she's not.

Considerate and tender. She will always strive to please her partner - and handle his tired body with patience. She's a dream come true for any man's ego.

CHAPTER 5

COMPATIBILITY QUIZ

Are you banging your head against the wall, or does she unleash your positive potential? Do you provoke her or bring out the best in her? Is she making you throw your arms into the air in exasperation, or do you feel inspired and complete in her company? Take the test to find out.

Question 1.
Do you regard flexibility as a strength?

A - Not necessarily. It can actually be a sign of weakness and insecurity.
B - Being flexible is very important. It allows you to get more out of life.
C - Flexibility can get you in touch with interesting people.

Question no 2
Do you think erotic fantasies make you a better lover?

A - Yes. Fantasies make you inherently more creative.
B - Nope! Daydreaming is nothing but a waste of time.
C - It may, provided the fantasies don't stay in your head.

(cont.)

Question no 3
What does sex mean to you?

A – Playfulness, romance and loads of fun.
B – Tenderness, affection and sensuality.
C – Pure physical pleasure.

Question no 4
Does it bother you when a woman is very sensitive and easily hurt?

A - Yes. I find it difficult to speak my mind with someone who might take things too personally.
B – Not really. I try not to step on anybody's toes anyway.
C - Not at all. I respect and love sensitive girls.

Question no 5
Do you enjoy an energetic partner, generally speaking?

A - Absolutely. Life is an adventure. Why waste it?
B – Not really. Women who need to be doing something all the time wear me out.
C - Yes, provided we can do things together.

Question no 6
You find yourself in bed with a woman who you initially thought was sweet and cuddly. How do you react when she turns out to be a red-hot lover?

A – I'm not into surprises – especially not in bed. It would put me off.
B - What more could a man ask for? I'd love it!
C – I'd be a little shocked, but I'm sure I'd enjoy it – and her!

Question no 7
Do you enjoy dating a woman who treats you like you're the only man in the world?

A - That depends on how much I like her. I don't want to feel cornered.
B - I don't like that. Freedom and independence are important – for both of us.
C - Of course. Who wouldn't want to be pampered with attention?

Question no 8
Do you find it easy to kiss and make up after a fight?

A – Unfortunately, no. I'm too proud.
B - No problem. What's the point of being angry for days?
C - Yes, but only if the forgiveness is mutual.

Question no 9
Do you tend to rush your partner when you're aroused?

A - Never. I believe in allowing things to develop at their own pace.
B - Sometimes, but only if I'm really hot.
C - Yes. What's the point of dragging things out when you're ready?

Question no 10
Is it important to you that a woman knows exactly what how to arouse and satisfy you?

A – Yes, of course. What's the point of having sex if she doesn't please me?
B - Not right away. Everybody needs a bit of time to get to know their partner's needs.
C - Although it would be nice, I can't expect my partner to be a mind-reader.

SCORE	A	B	C
Question 1	1	10	5
Question 2	10	1	5
Question 3	5	10	1
Question 4	1	5	10
Question 5	10	1	5
Question 6	1	10	5
Question 7	5	1	10
Question 8	1	10	5
Question 9	1	5	10
Question 10	10	1	5

75 – 100
All of a sudden the days are crackling with energy. Life feels comfortable and exciting – including your erotic life. The two of you know that sensuality is important. Since you share the same needs and values, you don't have to work too hard to achieve them. Sex will never be boring between you. You'll try a lot of different things, but never anything that could upset either of you. Keep going as you are, and this will grow into a happy, positive, caring and sensual relationship.

51 – 74
If you're not at home gazing into each other's eyes, you're probably out and about together, getting to know new people and visiting exciting places. Not only is your life going to be filled with exciting sex, it will be romantic, too. You'll never allow grey days or details ruin this wonderful relationship. Never mind silly arguments and stupid upsets; just let it slide and move on. Life is short, and the adventures to come are many. You both realise that in order to live life to the fullest, you'll need to communicate and be on the same level. Full steam ahead!

26 – 50
Well, this relationship has a bit of everything. Plenty of joy and excitement, but also moments of doubt and frustration. There's wonderful sex, but also times when you could do without the hassle. In short, you're facing a roller coaster of emotions, adventures, expectations – and disappointments. It can work. It can be great. Or it could be a pain – something that holds you both back. The keys to success are communication, understanding and mutual goals. If even talking about it is too much trouble, why delay the exit? If you don't do something, you'll both be completely drained before long.

10 – 25
Soft and sensitive. Cute, feminine and cuddly. Not really your thing, huh? She has many sides to her personality: she can be tough, firm and straight to the point – at least in her professional life. Her private and romantic life? Well, that's a different story. She is a flower, a poet and a delicate woman who needs careful attention. She wants a man to be a man. If you're not prepared to take on that responsibility, or if you want a strong woman who can boss you around a bit, you'll have to look somewhere else. Sure, you can try to talk it over, but at some point, you'll have to make up your mind.

Thoughts...
Her moods may confuse you a little at times - or maybe you are being insensitive to her needs without knowing.

Love rules. Embrace it.

...just a final note:
This book has not been approved by your date and should be treated accordingly. He or she *may* not agree with the content.

www.ingramcontent.com/pod-product-compliance
Lightning Source LLC
Chambersburg PA
CBHW071310150426
43191CB00007B/570